TEACHER'S G

VOICES of FREEDOM

English and Civics

Third Edition

Bill Bliss with **Steven J. Molinsky**

Carol H. Van Duzer • Deborah L. Schaffer

Longman

longman.com

MW00377396

Voices of Freedom: English and Civics, Third Edition

Pearson Education, 10 Bank Street, White Plains, NY 10606

Vice president, director of publishing: *Allen Ascher*
Editorial manager: *Pam Fishman*
Vice president, director of design and production: *Rhea Banker*
Director of electronic production: *Aliza Greenblatt*
Production manager: *Ray Keating*
Senior manufacturing manager: *Patrice Fraccio*
Manufacturing supervisor: *Dave Dickey*
Cover design: *Wendy Wolf*
Digital layout specialist: *Wendy Wolf*
Editorial supervisor: *Janet Johnston*

Photo credit: **Cover** www.comstock.com and Ed Pritchard/Stone/Getty Images.

ISBN: 0-13-045267-X

1 2 3 4 5 6 7 8 9 10–BAH–05 04 03 02 01 00

CONTENTS

TO THE TEACHER

Voices of Freedom is a content-based English and Civics text for beginning-level learners of English. It offers students a basic introduction to U.S. history and government and features activities designed to promote civic participation. The text is designed to serve as a simple English/Civics social studies course for adult and secondary-school learners as well as a preparatory course for students who will be applying for citizenship.

The text covers basic government and history topics through a carefully controlled sequence of lessons that simultaneously teach beginning-level vocabulary and grammar. It is specifically designed for students whose limited language skills prevent them from using standard social studies or civics materials. This third edition includes many new features suggested by users of the previous editions:

- Vocabulary preview sections at the beginning of each chapter
- Civic participation activities and issue discussions designed to meet English/Civics program goals
- Expanded chapter tests to develop students' test-taking skills
- Project-based activities to promote active learning and student teamwork
- Internet activities that range from simple web-browsing to virtual field trips to important historical sites
- Chapter summaries highlighting key vocabulary and grammar

Students also have many opportunities to share information about the government and history of their native countries. In this way, *Voices of Freedom* aims to give respect and attention to each student's country, history, and culture as the student learns about the government, history, and civic life of the United States.

In addition to the civics curriculum, *Voices of Freedom* offers students critically important practice using functional interview skills—the communication strategies they will need if they are preparing for an interview at an INS office.

The citizenship applicant's ability to handle the give-and-take of routine interview questions will often determine the INS examiner's assessment of English language ability. These strategies include Asking for Clarification; Asking for Repetition; Checking and Indicating Understanding; Correcting; Hesitating; and Reporting Personal Information.

INSTRUCTIONAL FORMATS AND ACTIVITIES

Voices of Freedom lessons provide the following types of activities:

Readings: Students are first introduced to basic information about government, history, and civics through short readings that are always accompanied by one or more photographs. The readings are designed for high readability by lowest-level students: they are printed in large-size type, each sentence appears on a separate line, and there is very generous spacing between lines and between paragraphs.

Interview Dialogs: These conversation practice activities provide students with authentic examples of the communication that occurs between an INS examiner and a citizenship applicant during an INS interview. These dialogs cover a wide range of topics, including personal identification, personal information about background and family, and question-and-answer exchanges about government, history, and civics. The interview dialogs provide crucial practice since an applicant's language ability will be assessed through the normal course of the interview.

Check-Up Exercises: These activities provide intensive skills practice in grammar, vocabulary, reading comprehension, and filling out forms. They essentially serve as a "workbook within the book" using standard exercise formats. To do these activities, students need little or no teacher instruction or supervision. The Check-Up Exercises are therefore very appropriate as homework.

"Questions & Answers" Activities: These unique lessons offer students critically important practice with the multiple ways a question might be posed by an INS examiner. Students first study various ways that a particular question might be worded, and then practice asking and answering questions with other students. In this way, students will not only know the answers, they will also "know the questions."

Listening Exercises: Each chapter offers students a listening activity, most of which require students to listen carefully for questions that sound the same or might otherwise be easily confused. Students are trained to listen closely to avoid mistakes they might make during an interview due to their misunderstanding of an examiner's question. For the teacher, scripts for the listening exercises appear at the back of the textbook and in the Teacher's Guide. All listening exercises are also included on the *Voices of Freedom* Audio Program.

Review Lessons: At the end of many chapters, students do one or more review exercises. These serve not only to review the content of the chapter but to cumulatively review content introduced earlier. Two unique formats for review activities are the "Information Exchange," in which students interview each other and record information collected during the interviews, and the "Talking Time Line," in which students match events with their dates, write the events on a time line, and then practice asking and answering questions based on the time line information.

Chapter Tests: Twenty-item multiple-choice tests at the end of each chapter evaluate student achievement of the chapter learning objectives while developing students' test-taking skills.

Dictation Exercises: At the end of each chapter test, students practice writing five sentences from dictation. This prepares them for the sentence-writing requirement during the INS examination. Scripts for the dictation exercises appear at the back of the book and in the Teacher's Guide.

Civics Enrichment Activities: New in the third edition, these activities at the end of each chapter promote students' active participation in class and in the civic life of the community.

Activities include:

CIVIC PARTICIPATION ACTIVITIES are designed to bring civics instruction alive by involving students in local government through visits to city hall and representatives' offices, attendance at local government or school board meetings, and classroom visits by local officials.

PROJECT ACTIVITIES enable students to work together in teams or as a class to decorate bulletin boards with civics content, create local maps, simulate an Election Day in class, or have a Thanksgiving celebration.

COMMUNITY ISSUES DISCUSSIONS encourage students to apply civics content to their own lives, to identify issues and problems related to their well-being in the community, and to brainstorm solutions.

DEBATES organize students into teams, each team taking one side of an issue and arguing positions in front of the class.

INTERNET ACTIVITIES use online resources to take virtual field trips to historic places, to visit the websites of government officials, and to do simple web-browsing tasks to find information.

100 Questions for Review: The text includes 100 common civics questions and answers arranged in a convenient double-column format, allowing students to use this section for practice as well as a self-check.

The Appendix: The appendix includes listening and dictation scripts, songs, the Oath of Allegiance that is recited at naturalization ceremonies, an index, and a correlation key that provides teachers with an easy resource for integrating the civics curriculum with lessons in the *Foundations*, *Side by Side*, *Word by Word*, and *ExpressWays* programs.

LOW BEGINNING-LEVEL STUDENTS

For students who are particularly low-level beginners, the first two preparatory chapters of *Voices of Freedom* have been designed to provide a solid, basic foundation in English communication and literacy. The chapters introduce the alphabet, numbers, and very basic vocabulary and expressions through the context of personal identification skills, in a format and a sequence that is appropriate for beginning-level students of English. The very easy exercise formats in these chapters, which involve circling, matching, and filling in boxes and blanks, are particularly designed to give low-level beginners a feeling of immediate success and momentum in their study of English and Civics. Students who already have some basic understanding of English can skip these preparatory chapters and begin their studies with Chapter One.

TEACHING TECHNIQUES

Voices of Freedom has been designed to be as easy-to-use as possible, for the teacher as well as the students. Exercise formats are simple and consistent so that students will need little or no explanation of how to complete the various activities.

Two of the central learning devices in the text are the readings and the interview dialogs. For these two types of activities, the following teaching steps are suggested. Teachers, however, should always feel free to use these activities in the way that is most appropriate for their teaching styles and their particular students.

Readings

1. Have students talk about the photograph and/or their own experiences in order to establish a context, or schema, for what they are about to read.

2. Have students read the story silently. (If you wish, you may read the story aloud or play the audio program as they read silently.)

3. Ask students a simple question about each line of the story. For low-level beginning students, ask the questions in the sequence of the story. For higher-level students, ask the questions out of sequence.

4. Ask students if they don't understand any vocabulary. Have students help define any unfamiliar words.

5. Do a choral repetition of the reading, line by line. (This is not reading practice, but is rather speaking practice. While such speaking practice is not usually done with a reading passage, it is appropriate in *Voices of Freedom* since each line of a reading is a possible answer to an INS examiner's question. This speaking practice prepares students for the interview dialog practice that will follow.)

6. Class Circle Reading. Have students read the passage as a class with different students reading each line in turn. You can assign who will read in a variety of ways: by seating patterns, by assigning each line of the passage, or by letting students take turns spontaneously.

7. Pair Practice. Have students work in pairs, reading the passage to each other paragraph by paragraph, for further speaking practice. Circulate around the room, checking students' reading and pronunciation, and focus more attention, if possible, on students who need more assistance.

8. When comprehension questions about the reading appear in the "Check-Up" exercises following a reading, have students first fill in their written answers, and then practice, in pairs, asking and answering these questions aloud.

Interview Dialogs

1. Set the scene. Have students look at the photograph and decide who the people are. You might simply mention in a word or two what they are talking about, such as "the flag" or "the Civil War."

2. Have students listen to the interview dialog with their books closed. Present the dialog yourself (taking both roles), present it with the help of another student, have two students present it to the rest of the class, or play the audio.

3. Choral Repetition. Have students repeat each line of the dialog in unison after you. (Books still closed.)

4. Have students open their books and look at the dialog. Ask if there are any questions about vocabulary.

5. Choral Conversation Practice.

   a. Divide the class into two groups (two halves or by rows). Have Group 1 say Speaker A's lines in unison, and have Group 2 say Speaker B's lines. Then reverse.

   and/or

   b. You say Speaker A's lines, and then the entire class says Speaker B's lines in unison. Then reverse.

6. Call on one or two pairs of students to present the dialog.

7. Pair Practice. Have students practice the dialog in pairs, taking turns being Speaker A and Speaker B. Encourage students to look at each other during the practice rather than "burying" their heads in the books. This will help their spoken language sound more authentic and conversational.

   (You can pair students in different ways. You can pair students of similar ability together and thereby focus your attention on those pairs of students who require more attention. Or you can pair weaker students with stronger ones so that your more-capable students have the opportunity to consolidate their skills while providing help to others in the class.)

Additional Communication Practice

Throughout *Voices of Freedom* there are many written exercises that include instructions to have students practice conversationally with another student. These include the "Questions and Answers" exercises, the "Information Exchange" activities, the "Talking Time Line" activities, and many of the review exercises. After students have completed the writing required for these exercises, whether at home or in class, they should practice asking and answering the questions aloud with another student. This additional speaking practice helps students consolidate their communication skills before moving on to the information to be presented in the succeeding lessons.

TEACHER'S GUIDE

This Teacher's Guide provides step-by-step teaching instructions for all lessons in *Voices of Freedom*. It also includes a variety of supplemental resources to help instructors integrate technology, prepare students for the INS interview, and assess student progress.

Technology Enrichment: A list of websites provides additional Internet resources that expand upon the topics in each chapter.

Needs Assessment Forms: These reproducible forms are designed to help programs or instructors gather input from students about their needs and interests in order to guide the development of instruction. A Pictorial Version provides a simple format for low-beginning-level students; a Checklist Version offers a more detailed format for students who have some reading ability.

Pre-Post Assessments: These reproducible knowledge/skill surveys may be used to evaluate students' prior knowledge and abilities before instruction as well as student achievement of learning objectives after instruction. Three pre-post assessments are provided, one for each third of the *Voices of Freedom* instructional program.

Performance-Based Assessment Records: These reproducible observation forms enable teachers to evaluate and document student participation and performance in each chapter's Civics Enrichment activities, which are designed to promote students' active participation in class and in the civic life of the community. Scoring rubrics guide the alternative assessment of these projects, issues discussions, community tasks, field trips, and Internet activities. The *Student Name List Mask* provides a convenient way to make a list of students' names and then affix it to each of the Assessment Record forms. The *Project Activity Observation Checklist* provides an assessment tool for evaluating students as they participate in all phases of a project and develop skills in leadership, teamwork, and communicating information—key workplace skills identified by the Secretary's Commission on Achieving Necessary Skills (SCANS).

Chapter Test Answer Sheet: This reproducible page offers a means for students to bubble in their answers to the twenty multiple-choice questions and to write the five dictation sentences in each chapter test. Using this, students practice the coordination skills involved in matching questions in a test booklet with the corresponding answer lines on a separate answer sheet.

The INS Interview: Information for Students: This section offers students helpful advice about what to expect at an INS interview and important practice with the types of questions about personal information and other topics that they may need to answer.

English & Civics Instruction Resources: A list of websites, print material, and videos provides teachers with resources for background information and instructional materials.

Correlation Key: A convenient chart indicates how to integrate the civics instruction in *Voices of Freedom* with the language instruction offered in *Side by Side*, *Foundations*, *Word by Word*, *Access*, and *ExpressWays*.

A FINAL WORD: THE "GOAL" OF CIVICS EDUCATION

At the beginning of the last century, the goal of citizenship education in so-called "Americanization" classes was to indoctrinate students with U.S. civics information in a way that often discredited their native countries and cultures. It was as though students had to renounce their backgrounds and heritages in order to acquire knowledge about their new country. In this new century, we aspire to a nobler effort: to offer students the language skills and civics knowledge they need to attain citizenship, to live full and productive lives, and to participate fully in the civic life of their communities and the country, and to do so through an educational program that recognizes and respects the diversity of cultures, histories, and experiences that our students bring to our classrooms . . . and the nation.

Bill Bliss

VOICES of FREEDOM
TEACHER'S GUIDE

<table>
<tr><td>

CHAPTER A

</td><td>

OVERVIEW
Student Text
Pages 1–18

</td></tr>
</table>

TOPICS

Personal Information
Identification Cards
Alphabet
Numbers

GRAMMAR

To Be
WH-Questions

FUNCTIONAL INTERVIEW SKILLS

Reporting Personal Information
Asking for Clarification

KEY VOCABULARY

PERSONAL INFORMATION

address
apartment
area code
avenue
city
country
county
family name
file number
first name
full name
given name
home
last name
middle name
name
number
phone
social security number
state
street
surname
telephone number
zip code

IDENTIFICATION CARDS

"A"-number
card
INS "A"-number
permanent resident card
social security card

IMMIGRATION STATUS

citizen
citizenship
permanent resident

FUNCTIONAL EXPRESSIONS

Could you spell that, please?
You mean . . . ?

OTHER WORDS

a	my
am	of
and	please
applying	spell
capital letters	that
daytime	the
enter	this
evening	United States
for	of America
from	want
I	what
I'm	work
include	yes
including	your
is	

NUMBERS

0	zero (oh)	7	seven	14	fourteen	30	thirty
1	one	8	eight	15	fifteen	40	forty
2	two	9	nine	16	sixteen	50	fifty
3	three	10	ten	17	seventeen	60	sixty
4	four	11	eleven	18	eighteen	70	seventy
5	five	12	twelve	19	nineteen	80	eighty
6	six	13	thirteen	20	twenty	90	ninety

RELATED PRACTICE

Foundations: Chapter 1
Word by Word Basic: pages 2–7, 48, 54–55
Word by Word: pages 1–3, 30, 33
Side by Side Book 1: Chapters 1–3
Side by Side Interactive CD-ROM / Side by Side TV Video: Level 1A, Segments 1–4
ExpressWays Book 1: Chapter 1
Access: Chapters 1, 2

TEXT PAGE 1: *Vocabulary Preview*

You may want to introduce these words before beginning the chapter, or you may choose to wait until they first occur in a specific lesson. If you choose to introduce them at this point, here are some suggestions:

1. Have students look at the permanent resident card and the social security card on text page 1 and identify the words they already know.

2. Present the vocabulary. Say each word and have the class repeat it chorally and individually. Check students' understanding and pronunciation of the words.

3. Practice the vocabulary as a class, in pairs, or in small groups. Have students cover the word list and look at the permanent resident card and the social security card. Practice the words in the following ways:

   • Say a word and have students tell the number of that word on the illustration.
   • Give the number of an item in an illustration and have students say the word.

TEXT PAGE 2: *Applying for Citizenship*

FOCUS

> ### TOPIC
> Personal Information
>
> ### GRAMMAR
>
> **To Be**
>
> My name **is** Carlos Rivera.
> **I'm** a permanent resident.

NEW VOCABULARY

a	I
applying	I'm
citizen	is
citizenship	last name
first name	my
for	name
	permanent resident
	United States of America
	want

GETTING READY

1. Introduce *name, first name,* and *last name.*

   a. Write your first and last name on the board.

   b. Point to your name and say, "My name is _____."

   c. Point to your first name and say, "My first name is _____."

   d. Point to your last name and say, "My last name is _____."

   e. Ask individual students:

   > "What's your name?"
   > "What's your first name?"
   > "What's your last name?"

2. Introduce the following forms of the verb **To Be.**

   > **am**   **I'm** a permanent resident.
   > **is**   My name **is** Carlos Rivera.

PREVIEWING THE STORY

Have students talk about the story title and the photograph to establish the context of the story. Ask some or all of the following questions:

> Where is he going? (Into an INS office.)
> Why? (He's applying for citizenship.)
> Where is he from? (Have students guess.)
> Is he happy? nervous? Why?
> Are *you* a permanent resident?
> Are *you* applying for citizenship?

READING THE STORY

1. Have students read the story silently.

2. **Check reading comprehension:** Ask students a question about each line of the story. For beginning-level students, ask these questions in the order below so that the questions follow the sequence of the story. For higher-level students, ask the questions in random order.

   > What's his name?
   > What's his first name?
   > What's his last name?
   >
   > What is he?
   > What's he applying for?
   > What does he want to be?

3. Ask students if they have any questions about the story; check understanding of vocabulary.

4. **Choral Repetition:** Read aloud each line of the story and have students repeat.

5. **Class Circle Reading:** Have students read the story aloud as a class, with different students reading each line. (You can assign each line to a particular student or by seating patterns, or by letting students take turns spontaneously. In large classes, have a different group or row of students read each line.)

6. **Pair Practice:** Have students work in pairs, reading the passage to each other, paragraph by paragraph. Circulate around the room and check students' reading and pronunciation, focusing more attention on students who need more assistance.

EXPANSION

Introducing Oneself

Have students walk around the class introducing themselves to each other. Participate in the activity yourself to encourage students to feel comfortable.

TEXT PAGE 3: *Check-Up*

CIRCLE THE SAME WORD

This activity serves as a diagnostic check of students' basic literacy skills. Students need to be able to identify the word that is the same as the word on the left. Do the first two exercises with students to be sure they understand the instructions. Students who have difficulty with this activity should be offered the basic literacy instruction provided in *ACCESS: Fundamentals of Literacy and Communication* as they cover the early chapters of *Voices of Freedom*.

1. name
2. My
3. last
4. citizen
5. first
6. permanent

VOCABULARY CHECK

1. name
2. citizenship
3. last
4. permanent
5. applying

HOW ABOUT YOU?

Have students write their first and last names on the blank lines. For low-beginning-level students, you might want to have students copy their first and last names from their permanent resident cards, from other identification cards, or from a model provided by you.

TEXT PAGE 4: *Permanent Resident Card*

FOCUS

TOPICS

Personal Information
Identification Cards

GRAMMAR

To Be

This **is** my permanent resident card.

NEW VOCABULARY

card	middle name
family name	surname
full name	this
given name	

GETTING READY

Introduce *given name, middle name, family name, surname,* and *full name.*

  a. Write your full name on the board.

  b. Point to your first name and say, "My first name is _____," "My given name is _____."

  c. Point to your middle name and say, "My middle name is _____."

  d. Point to your last name and say, "My last name is _____," "My family name is _____," "My surname is _____."

  e. Point to your full name and say, "My full name is _____."

  f. Ask individual students:

    "What's your first name / given name?"
    "What's your middle name?"
    "What's your last name / family name / surname?"
    "What's your full name?"

PREVIEWING THE STORY

Have students talk about the story title and the illustration to establish the context of the story. Ask some or all of the following questions:

  What's this card? (Permanent resident card.)
  What's his name? (Carlos Manuel Rivera.)
  What's the mark on the right? (Fingerprint.)
  Do you have a permanent resident card? (Have students display their cards and point to their names on the cards.)

READING THE STORY

1. Have students read the story silently.

2. **Check reading comprehension:** Ask students a question about each line of the story. For beginning-level students, ask these questions in the order below so that the questions follow the sequence of the story. For higher-level students, ask the questions in random order.

   What is he?
   What is this?

   What's his last name?
   What's his first name?
   What's his middle name?
   What's his full name?

   What's he applying for?
   What does he want to be?

   To practice the other terms for names, also ask:

   What's his family name?
   What's his surname?
   What's his given name?

3. Ask students if they have any questions about the story; check understanding of vocabulary.

4. **Choral Repetition:** Read aloud each line of the story and have students repeat.

5. **Class Circle Reading:** Have students read the story aloud as a class, with different students reading each line. (You can assign each line to a particular student or by seating patterns, or by letting students take turns spontaneously. In large classes, have a different group or row of students read each line.)

6. **Pair Practice:** Have students work in pairs, reading the passage to each other, paragraph by paragraph. Circulate around the room and check students' reading and pronunciation, focusing more attention on students who need more assistance.

EXPANSION

Roleplay: Identifying Oneself

a. Set the scene: Tell the class, "You're at the INS office."

b. Have pairs of students come to the front of the class. Have one student say, "What's your name?" Have the other student say, "My name is _____. This is my permanent resident card."

TEXT PAGE 5: *Check-Up*

GRAMMAR CHECK

1. is
2. My
3. a
4. I'm
5. want

FILL OUT THE FORM

This exercise offers students practice with a simulated section of an INS form. Have students write their own names as requested. Low-beginning-level students may need to copy this information from a model.

WHAT'S YOUR NAME?

Have students print their first, middle, and last names on the blank lines for Exercises 1–3 and in the boxes for Exercise 4. Low-beginning-level students may need to copy this information from a model. Point out to students that "last name," "family name," and "surname" are synonymous, and so are "first name" and "given name."

FOCUS

TOPICS

Personal Information
Alphabet

GRAMMAR

WH-Questions

What's your family name?

To Be

What's your first name?

FUNCTIONAL INTERVIEW SKILL

Reporting Personal Information

NEW VOCABULARY

and	what
please	your
spell	Could you spell
that	that, please?

GETTING READY

Introduce the alphabet.

a. Use flash cards or write the letter A on the board. Have students repeat, "A."

b. Next to A, use the flash card B or write the letter B. Have students repeat, "A, B."

c. Continue with the letters C, D, and E.

d. Next, point to these letters at random. Have students say the letters.

e. Continue the above steps with groups of five or six letters at a time until you have completed the alphabet.

f. Have the class repeat the alphabet.

PRACTICING THE MODEL DIALOG

1. **Setting the Scene:** Have students look at the photograph and determine who is talking: an INS examiner and an applicant. Establish the context: "The INS examiner is asking questions about the applicant's name."

2. **Listening:** With books closed, have students listen to the dialog—presented by you, by a pair of students, or on the audio program.

3. **Choral Repetition:** With books still closed, model each line and have the whole class repeat in unison.

4. **Reading:** With books open, have students follow along as two students present the model dialog. Ask students if they have any questions and check understanding of vocabulary.

5. **Choral Conversation Practice:** Divide the class in half. Have Group 1 ask the questions and Group 2 give the answers; then reverse. (Or: You ask the questions and have the whole class answer in unison; then reverse.)

6. Call on one or two pairs of students to present the model dialog.

PRACTICING NEW DIALOGS

1. Call on one or two pairs of students to present new dialogs, using the skeletal dialog as a guide and filling in the blanks with the appropriate information.

2. **Pair Practice:** Have students practice making new dialogs in pairs, taking turns being the INS examiner and the applicant.

3. Call on one or two more pairs of students to present their new dialogs to the class.

EXPANSION

"Alphabet Soup" Game

a. Write the 26 letters of the alphabet randomly on the board, or use flash cards.

b. Divide the class into teams.

c. Point to a letter or show a flash card. The first player on Team 1 says the letter. The team gets a point for a correct answer.

d. Show a different letter to the first player on Team 2. If the answer is incorrect, show the same letter to the second player on Team 1 or the first player on Team 3.

e. The team with the most correct answers wins.

ALPHABET PRACTICE

1. A, E, M, N
   NAME

2. A, C, D, R
   CARD

3. A, L, S, T
   LAST

4. A, F, I, L, M, Y
   FAMILY

LISTENING

Have students complete the exercises as you play the audio program or read the following:

Listen and circle the correct answer.

1. A. Could you spell your family name, please?
   B. M-A-R-T-I-N-E-Z.

2. A. Could you spell your last name, please?
   B. S-A-N-T-O-S.

3. A. Could you spell your surname, please?
   B. T-R-A-N.

4. A. How do you spell your last name?
   B. C-R-U-Z.

5. A. How do you spell your family name?
   B. W-O-N-G.

Listen and write the name you hear.

1. A. What's your family name?
   B. Garcia.
   A. Could you spell that, please?
   B. G-A-R-C-I-A.

2. A. What's your last name?
   B. Lam.
   A. Could you spell that, please?
   B. L-A-M.

3. A. What's your surname?
   B. Perez.
   A. Could you spell that, please?
   B. P-E-R-E-Z.

4. A. What's your last name?
   B. Cheng.
   A. How do you spell that?
   B. C-H-E-N-G.

5. A. What's your family name?
   B. Velasquez.
   A. How do you spell that?
   B. V-E-L-A-S-Q-U-E-Z.

6. A. What's your surname?
   B. Gudarski.
   A. Please spell it.
   B. G-U-D-A-R-S-K-I.

Answers

1. Martinez
2. Santos
3. Tran
4. Cruz
5. Wong

1. Garcia	4. Cheng
2. Lam	5. Velasquez
3. Perez	6. Gudarski

TEXT PAGE 8: *Numbers*

FOCUS

TOPICS
Identification Cards
Numbers

GRAMMAR

To Be

My "A"-number **is** A-92475816.

NEW VOCABULARY

number	zero (oh)	five
"A"-number	one	six
social security card	two	seven
social security number	three	eight
telephone number	four	nine

GETTING READY

Teach the numbers 0–9.

   a. Write 0 on the board. Say "zero" and have students repeat.

   b. Next to 0 write 1. Say "one" and have students repeat.

   c. Point to 0 and 1 on the board as you say "zero, one" and have students repeat.

   d. Introduce the numbers 2, 3, and 4, using steps b and c.

   e. Point to these numbers at random and have the class say them.

   f. Continue the above steps with the numbers 5–9.

   g. Have the class count from 0 to 9.

   h. Have individual students count from 0 to 9.

PREVIEWING THE STORY

Have students talk about the story title and the illustrations to establish the context of the story. Ask some or all of the following questions:

   What are these cards? (permanent resident card/social security card.)
   Do *you* have a permanent resident card? (Have students show their cards.)

What's this number? (Point to the "A"-number.)
Point to *your* A-number on *your* card.
What's your "A"-number?
Do *you* have a social security card? (Have students show their cards.)
What's this number? (Point to the social security number.)
Point to *your* social security number on *your* card.
What's your social security number?

(Point to the third illustration on the page.)
What's this? (A telephone number/a telephone listing.)
Where is it? (In a telephone book.)
Do *you* have a telephone?
What's your telephone number?

READING THE STORY

1. Have students read the story silently.

2. **Check reading comprehension:** Ask students a question about each line of the story. For beginning-level students, ask these questions in the order below so that the questions follow the sequence of the story. For higher-level students, ask the questions in random order.

   What's this card?
   What's his "A"-number?

   What's this card?
   What's his social security number?

   What kind of number is this?
   What's his telephone number?

3. Ask students if they have any questions about the story; check understanding of vocabulary.

4. **Choral Repetition:** Read aloud each line of the story and have students repeat.

5. **Class Circle Reading:** Have students read the story aloud as a class, with different students reading each line. (You can assign each line to a particular student or by seating patterns, or by letting students take turns spontaneously. In large classes, have a different group or row of students read each line.)

6. **Pair Practice:** Have students work in pairs, reading the passage to each other, paragraph by paragraph. Circulate around the room and check students' reading and pronunciation, focusing more attention on students who need more assistance.

EXPANSION

1. Number Clapping

a. Clap your hands or tap on the desk. Have students respond by saying the number of claps.

b. Have a student clap or tap. Have the other students respond.

2. Interviews

a. On the board, write:

last name
first name
telephone number
social security number

b. Ask, "What's your last name?" Have a student answer.

c. Ask, "Could you spell that, please?" Write the name on the board as the student spells it.

d. Continue with first name, using steps b and c.

e. Ask, "What's your telephone number?" Write the number.

f. Ask, "What's your social security number?" Write the number.

g. In pairs, have students ask for and write the information about each other.

TEXT PAGE 9: *Check-Up*

MATCHING

Have students draw a line from the words on the left to the corresponding information on the right.

1. Carlos Rivera
2. (213) 257-9108
3. 408-37-1692
4. A-92475816

ANSWER THESE QUESTIONS

New Vocabulary: area code, home, include, phone, work

Have students answer the questions with their own information. Low-beginning-level students may need to copy this information from a model.

(Note: An "A"-number can have seven, eight, or nine digits, depending on when it was issued by the INS. Students with seven-digit numbers need to put two zero [0] numbers before their "A"-number when they fill out INS forms. Students with eight-digit numbers need to put one zero [0] number before the "A"-number.)

FILL OUT THE FORM

New Vocabulary: daytime phone number, evening phone number

This exercise offers students practice with a simulated section of an INS form. Have students provide the information as requested on the form. Low-beginning-level students may need to copy the information from a model. Make sure students write in capital letters.

TEXT PAGE 10: *My Address*

FOCUS

> **TOPIC**
>
> Personal Information
>
> **GRAMMAR**
>
> **To Be**
>
> My address **is** 80 Stanley Avenue.

NEW VOCABULARY

address	ten	twenty
apartment	eleven	thirty
avenue	twelve	forty
city	thirteen	fifty
of	fourteen	sixty
state	fifteen	seventy
the	sixteen	eighty
United States	seventeen	ninety
of America	eighteen	
zip code	nineteen	

GETTING READY

1. Teach the numbers 10–100.

   a. Review the numbers 0–9.

   b. Write 10 on the board. Say "ten" and have students repeat.

   c. Next to 10 write 11. Say "eleven" and have students repeat.

   d. Point to 10 and 11 on the board as you say "ten, eleven" and have students repeat.

   e. Introduce the numbers 12–19, using steps c and d.

   f. Erase the board and have individual students count from 0 to 19.

   g. Write 20 on the board. Say "twenty" and have students repeat.

   h. Write 21–29 on the board. Count from 21 to 29 and have students repeat number by number.

   i. Have individual students count from 0 to 29.

   j. Write 30 on the board. Say "thirty" and have students repeat.

   k. Write 40, say "forty," and have students repeat.

   l. Point to 30 and 40 as you say "thirty, forty" and have students repeat.

   m. Continue through 100, using steps k and l.

   n. Write numbers randomly on the board. Have the class read them. Then have individual students read them. For example, "36, 43, 51, 27, 89."

2. Introduce addresses.

   Write a local address on the board and point out each part. For example, "This is the building number. This is the street number." Do this for city, state, and zip code.

PREVIEWING THE STORY

Have students talk about the story title and the photograph to establish the context of the story. Ask some or all of the following questions:

> Where is he? (Inside INS.)
> Why? (He's applying for citizenship.)
> What is he saying/thinking? (Students guess.)

READING THE STORY

1. Have students read the story silently.

2. **Check reading comprehension:** Ask students a question about each line of the story. For beginning-level students, ask these questions in the order below so that the questions follow the sequence of the story. For higher-level students, ask the questions in random order.

   > What's his address?
   > What's his apartment number?
   > What's the name of his city?
   > What's the name of his state?
   > Where is California?
   > What's his zip code?

3. Ask students if they have any questions about the story; check understanding of vocabulary.

4. **Choral Repetition:** Read aloud each line of the story and have students repeat.

5. **Class Circle Reading:** Have students read the story aloud as a class, with different students reading each line. (You can assign each line to a particular student or by seating patterns, or by letting students take turns spontaneously. In large classes, have a different group or row of students read each line.)

6. **Pair Practice:** Have students work in pairs, reading the passage to each other line by line. Circulate around the room and check students' reading and pronunciation, focusing more attention on students who need more assistance.

HOW ABOUT YOU?

Have students practice completing the sentences with their personal information.

EXPANSION

1. Interviews

a. Write on the board:

last name
first name
address

b. Ask, "What's your last name?" Have a student answer.

c. Ask, "Could you spell that, please?" Write the name on the board as the student spells it.

d. Continue with first name.

e. Ask, "What's your address?" Write the address.

f. In pairs, have students ask for and write the information about each other.

2. Reading Maps

Using a map of the United States showing cities and states, have students identify cities and states where they have visited or lived.

3. Addressing Envelopes

Have students address envelopes to relatives or friends who live in another city or state. (Let students take these envelopes home to use for mailing letters to the addressees.)

TEXT PAGE 11: *Check-Up*

MATCHING

1. (213) 257-9108
2. California
3. 90048
4. Los Angeles
5. 80 Stanley Avenue
6. #12-D

READING ADDRESSES

New Vocabulary: street

Have students practice reading addresses. Note that there are two ways to say a three-digit building number. Four-digit building numbers are said as two separate two-digit numbers.

LISTENING

Have students complete the exercises as you play the audio program or read the following:

Listen and circle the number you hear.

1. My address is thirty Main Street.
2. My address is thirteen Spring Street.
3. My address is fifty Stanley Avenue.
4. My address is forty-six fifteen Donaldson Street.
5. My address is eighteen thirty-nine Parkman Avenue.
6. My address is eight forty-two Conway Avenue.

Answers

1.	30	4.	4615
2.	13	5.	1839
3.	50	6.	842

TEXT PAGES 12–13: INTERVIEW: *What's Your File Number?*

FOCUS

TOPIC
Personal Information

GRAMMAR

To Be

What's your file number?

WH-Questions

What's the name of your state?

FUNCTIONAL INTERVIEW SKILLS

Reporting Personal Information
Asking for Clarification

NEW VOCABULARY

file number	You mean . . . ?
including	
yes	

PRACTICING THE MODEL DIALOG

1. **Setting the Scene:** Have students look at the photograph and determine who is talking: an INS examiner and an applicant. Establish the context: "The INS examiner is asking the applicant for information."

2. **Listening:** With books closed, have students listen to the dialog—presented by you, by a pair of students, or on the audio program.

3. **Choral Repetition:** With books still closed, model each line and have the whole class repeat in unison.

4. **Reading:** With books open, have students follow along as two students present the model dialog. Ask students if they have any questions and check understanding of vocabulary.

5. **Choral Conversation Practice:** Divide the class in half. Have Group 1 ask the questions and Group 2 give the answers; then reverse. (Or: You ask the questions and have the whole class answer in unison; then reverse.)

6. Call on one or two pairs of students to present the model dialog.

PRACTICING NEW DIALOGS

1. Call on one or two pairs of students to present new dialogs, using the skeletal dialog as a guide and filling in the blanks with the appropriate information.

2. **Pair Practice:** Have students practice making new dialogs in pairs, taking turns being the INS examiner and the applicant.

3. Call on one or two pairs of students to present their new dialogs to the class.

TEXT PAGE 14: *Check-Up*

WRITE YOUR HOME ADDRESS

Have students practice writing their complete home address three times to practice with these different styles of forms.

FILL OUT THE FORM

Have students practice writing the complete information requested on this simulated section of an INS form.

TEXT PAGE 15: *Information Exchange*

Have the entire class practice asking the questions in the box at the top of the page. Then have each student interview another student and write the information in the appropriate place on the form.

(For additional speaking practice, students can later report back to the class and tell about the student they interviewed.)

You can use this test as a standardized form of assessment to measure student achievement of the curriculum objectives in Chapter A. The test consists of 20 multiple-choice items and five sentences for dictation.

To score the test on a scale of 100:

- For each correct multiple-choice item, score four points.

- For each dictation sentence, do a general evaluation of the correctness of words, spelling, punctuation, and legibility. Score each sentence as follows:

  4 (Excellent), **3** (Good), **2** (Fair), **1** (Poor), **0** (Unsatisfactory)

Students can write their answers in the text or on the reproducible Chapter Test Answer Sheet provided in the Appendix.

A. PERSONAL INFORMATION

1. D
2. C
3. A
4. B
5. D
6. B
7. C
8. A
9. B
10. D
11. D
12. C

B. VOCABULARY

13. D
14. B
15. A
16. B
17. D
18. C
19. A
20. C

C. DICTATION

Have students write these sentences as you read each sentence twice or play the audio program:

1. My name is _____.
2. This is my home.
3. This is my address.
4. The United States is my new home.
5. I want to be a citizen.

TEXT PAGE 18: *Civics Enrichment*

PERFORMANCE-BASED ASSESSMENT

These civics enrichment activities are designed to promote students' active participation in class and in the civic life of the community—through projects, issues discussions, community tasks, field trips, and Internet activities. Reproducible performance-based assessment forms for use in evaluating and documenting student participation in these activities are included in the Appendix.

CIVIC PARTICIPATION

Have students discuss other forms of personal identification besides permanent resident cards and social security cards—driver's licenses, passports, state identification cards, school identification cards, and other documents. Have them discuss the kinds of identification they have, why forms of personal identification are important, and where they get them.

PROJECT ACTIVITY

In this project, students make a list of emergency telephone numbers for their community. They need to find out the information, create a list (or perhaps a more attractive brochure page with pictures or icons of the emergencies), make copies, and distribute them to all students so that they can be posted near the telephone in each student's home. Have students take responsibility for all aspects of this project. Have them identify the particular tasks involved in the project, who will accomplish each task, what resources are needed, and what form the final product will take. Use the project as a basis for building students' skills in leadership, teamwork, and acquiring, evaluating, and communicating information—key SCANS* skills useful for success in the workplace.

*Secretary's Commission on Achieving Necessary Skills

COMMUNITY ISSUES

Problem-Posing Discussion: Have students discuss whether it is difficult to use emergency services in their community, and have them discuss any reasons for this. (Students commonly describe long waiting times for the arrival of emergency personnel in their neighborhoods, the uncertainty of when it is appropriate to dial 911 and when it isn't considered necessary, and their concern about the expense of emergency ambulance services. From the viewpoint of emergency services personnel, some students and their families misuse ambulance services by calling them in situations that are not life-threatening, while others may not think to use emergency services in situations that require them.) Have students identify key issues and problems and share ideas about how to solve them.

<table>
<tr><td>

CHAPTER B

</td><td>

OVERVIEW
Student Text
Pages 19–34

</td></tr>
</table>

TOPICS

Personal Information
Months of the Year
Dates

GRAMMAR

To Be
WH-Questions
Yes/No Questions
Short Answers

FUNCTIONAL INTERVIEW SKILLS

Reporting Personal Information
Asking for Repetition
Checking and Indicating Understanding
Verifying Information
Correcting

KEY VOCABULARY

PERSONAL INFORMATION

address
area code
birth
birth date
born
city
country
country of birth
country of nationality
current address
date
date of birth
family name
first name
home address

home telephone number
information
maiden name
middle name
name
nationality
native country
place of birth
social security number
state
street
telephone number
town
work phone number
zip code

FAMILY MEMBERS

father
mother
parents

TIME EXPRESSIONS

date
day
month
year

IMMIGRATION STATUS

citizen
citizenship
naturalization
permanent resident
U.S. citizen

MONTHS

January
February
March
April
May
June
July
August
September
October
November
December

FUNCTIONAL EXPRESSIONS

All right.
Could you please say that again?
Excuse me?
I didn't understand.

I'm sorry.
Is that correct?
That's right.
Let me . . .

RELATED PRACTICE

Foundations: Chapter 1
Word by Word Basic: pages 2–7, 48, 54–55
Word by Word: pages 1–3, 30, 33
Side by Side Book 1: Chapters 4–6
Side by Side Interactive CD-ROM / Side by Side TV Video: Level 1A, Segments 5–8
ExpressWays Book 1: Chapter 1
Access: Chapters 3, 4

TEXT PAGE 19: *Vocabulary Preview*

You may want to introduce these words before beginning the chapter, or you may choose to wait until they first occur in a specific lesson. If you choose to introduce them at this point, here are some suggestions:

1. Have students look at the calendar and the date on text page 19. Have them identify the months they already know, and have them identify the parts of the date (month, day, year) they already know.

2. Present the vocabulary. Say each word and have the class repeat it chorally and individually. Check students' understanding and pronunciation of the words.

3. Practice the vocabulary as a class, in pairs, or in small groups. Have students cover the word list and look at the calendar and the date. Practice the words in the following ways:

   • Say a word and have students tell the number of that word in the illustration.
   • Give the number of a month on the calendar or the number of a part of the date and have students say the word.

TEXT PAGE 20: *I Was Born in Monterrey*

FOCUS

TOPICS

Reporting Personal Information
Months of the Year
Dates

GRAMMAR

To Be

My name **is** Maria Lopez.
I'm from Mexico.
My mother and father **are** in Monterrey.

NEW VOCABULARY

are	May	now
born	Mexican	on
father	mother	was
in	naturalization	

GETTING READY

Introduce dates.

Show a calendar. Point to today's date and say, "Today is *(month) (date), (year)*." For example, "Today is December 12, 2002."

PREVIEWING THE STORY

Have students talk about the story title and the photograph to establish the context of the story. Ask some or all of the following questions:

What country do you think she is from?
Where is she living now?
Where do you think she is in this photograph?
Why do you think she's smiling?

What's the name of our city?
What's the name of our state?
What's the name of our country?
What country are you from?

READING THE STORY

1. Have students read the story silently.

2. **Check Reading Comprehension:** Ask students a question about each line of the story. For beginning-level students, ask these questions in the order below so that the questions follow the sequence of the story. For higher-level students, ask the questions in random order.

   What's her name?
   Where is she from?
   Where is she now?
   What's the name of her city?
   Where is Houston?
   What is Texas?

   What nationality is she?
   Where was she born?
   Where is Monterrey?
   Where is Nuevo León?

   When was she born?
   What's her mother's name?
   What's her father's name?
   Where are her mother and father?

   What's she applying for?
   What does she want to be?

3. Ask students if they have any questions about the story; check understanding of vocabulary.

4. **Choral Repetition:** Read aloud each line of the story and have students repeat.

5. **Class Circle Reading:** Have students read the story aloud as a class, with different students reading each line. (You can assign each line to a particular student or by seating patterns, or by letting students take turns spontaneously. In large classes, have a different group or row of students read each line.)

6. **Pair Practice:** Have students work in pairs, reading the passage to each other paragraph by paragraph. Circulate around the room and check students' reading and pronunciation, focusing more attention on students who need more assistance.

TEXT PAGE 21: *Check-Up*

MATCHING

> 1. Maria Lopez.
> 2. Mexican.
> 3. Monterrey.
> 4. May 4, 1972.
> 5. naturalization.

VOCABULARY CHECK

> 1. name
> 2. city
> 3. state
> 4. born
> 5. mother
> 6. applying

FILL OUT THE FORM

New Vocabulary: country of birth, date of birth, day, month, year

This exercise offers students practice with a simulated section of an INS form. Have students fill in the boxes with their own information. Make sure that each student knows how to fill in his or her date of birth. Low-beginning-level students may need to copy this information from a model.

SHARING

Have students bring in photographs of family members. Have them describe their pictures by saying, "This is my _____. His/her name is _____. He/she is in _____." Teach words for other family members as necessary.

TEXT PAGE 22: INTERVIEW: *What's Your Place of Birth?*

FOCUS

> ### TOPIC
> Personal Information
>
> ### GRAMMAR
>
> #### WH-Questions
>
> **What**'s your place of birth?
> **Where** were you born?
>
> ### FUNCTIONAL INTERVIEW SKILLS
>
> Reporting Personal Information
> Asking for Repetition

NEW VOCABULARY

> | | |
> |---|---|
> | city | town |
> | native country | were |
> | or | where |
> | place of birth | Excuse me? |

PRACTICING THE MODEL DIALOG

1. **Setting the Scene:** Have students look at the photograph and determine who is talking: an INS examiner and an applicant. Establish the context: "The INS examiner is asking about where the applicant was born."

2. **Listening:** With books closed, have students listen to the dialog—presented by you, by a pair of students, or on the audio program.

3. **Choral Repetition:** With books still closed, model each line and have the whole class repeat in unison.

4. **Reading:** With books open, have students follow along as two students present the model dialog. Ask students if they have any questions and check understanding of vocabulary.

5. **Choral Conversation Practice:** Divide the class in half. Have Group 1 ask the questions and Group 2 give the answers; then reverse. (Or: You ask the questions and have the whole class answer in unison; then reverse.)

6. Call on one or two pairs of students to present the model dialog.

PRACTICING NEW DIALOGS

1. Call on one or two pairs of students to present new dialogs, using the skeletal dialog as a guide and filling in the blanks with the appropriate information.

2. **Pair Practice:** Have students practice making new dialogs in pairs, taking turns being the INS examiner and the applicant.

3. Call on one or two more pairs of students to present their new dialogs to the class.

EXPANSION

Bring in a world map. Have students point to where they were born and report the information to the class.

TEXT PAGE 23: *Check-Up*

QUESTIONS AND ANSWERS

This exercise offers students important practice with the multiple ways a question might be posed by the INS examiner. First, have students repeat each question after you. Then, have students practice asking and answering the questions with other students. Finally, have students write their answers to questions 1, 2, and 3.

MAP ACTIVITY

Have students bring in maps of their native countries, show where they were born, and tell about those places.

GRAMMAR CHECK

```
1. What
2. Where
3. What
4. What
5. Where
```

FOCUS

TOPICS

Personal Information
Months of the Year
Dates

GRAMMAR

WH-Questions

What's your date of birth?
When were you born?

FUNCTIONAL INTERVIEW SKILLS

Reporting Personal Information
Asking for Repetition
Checking and Indicating Understanding

NEW VOCABULARY

again	January	July
didn't	February	August
say	March	September
understand	April	October
when	May	November
	June	December

Could you please say that again?
I didn't understand.
I'm sorry.
That's right.

GETTING READY

1. Use a calendar to introduce the months of the year.

   a. Point to January on the calendar. Say "January" and have students repeat.

   b. Continue with all twelve months.

2. Practice dates.

   a. Tell students when your birthday is. Say, "I was born on *(month) (day)*."

   b. Ask a student, "When were you born?"

   c. Write that student's birthday on the board—for example, June 9. Have that student ask another student.

   d. Continue by having students ask each other. Write the dates on the board.

   e. Have students practice saying their birth dates. Teach each student how to say the ordinal number in the student's birth date.

PRACTICING THE MODEL DIALOG

1. **Setting the Scene:** Have students look at the photograph and determine who is talking: an INS examiner and an applicant. Establish the context: "The INS examiner is asking about the applicant's birth date."

2. **Listening:** With books closed, have students listen to the dialog—presented by you, by a pair of students, or on the audio program.

3. **Choral Repetition:** With books still closed, model each line and have the whole class repeat in unison.

4. **Reading:** With books open, have students follow along as two students present the model dialog. Ask students if they have any questions and check understanding of vocabulary.

5. **Choral Conversation Practice:** Divide the class in half. Have Group 1 ask the questions and Group 2 give the answers; then reverse. (Or: You ask the questions and have the whole class answer in unison; then reverse.)

6. Call on one or two pairs of students to present the model dialog.

PRACTICING NEW DIALOGS

1. Call on one or two pairs of students to present new dialogs, using the skeletal dialog as a guide and filling in the blanks with the appropriate information.

2. **Pair Practice:** Have students practice making new dialogs in pairs, taking turns being the INS examiner and the applicant.

3. Call on one or two more pairs of students to present their new dialogs to the class.

EXPANSION

1. Birthday Line-up

Tell students to line up in the order of their birthdays (month and day). The students will have to talk among themselves to determine who should be first, second, third, etc.

2. Working with Calendars

Have students fill in calendars with information about holidays and students' birthdays. (You can often get free calendar books at gift and card shops, or students can make their own.)

a. Ask students:

> Are there any American holidays in January?
> What's the date?

> Are there any holidays in your native country in January?
> What's the date?
> Do any students have birthdays in January?
> What's the date?

Have students record this information on their calendars.

b. Follow the same procedure for the other months.

TEXT PAGE 25: *Check-Up*

MONTHS AND YEARS

Say the months of the year and have students repeat. Then, model for students how to read the years listed in the second box.

QUESTIONS AND ANSWERS

This exercise offers students important practice with the multiple ways a question might be posed by the INS examiner. First, have students repeat each question after you. Then, have students practice asking and answering the questions with other students. Finally, have students write their answers to questions 1, 2, and 3.

CALENDAR ACTIVITY

Have students ask each other about birthdays, U.S. holidays, and native country holidays. Have students write these dates on their calendars. (If they have done the expansion activity with calendars for page 25, they can add these dates to the calendars.)

Are You Still Living at 86 Central Avenue?

FOCUS

> ### TOPIC
> Personal Information
>
> ### GRAMMAR
>
> **Yes/No Questions**
>
> **Are** you still living at 86 Central Avenue?
> **Is** your zip code 10715?
>
> **Short Answers**
>
> **Yes, I am.**
> **No, I'm not.**
>
> **Yes, it is.**
> **No, it isn't.**
>
> ### FUNCTIONAL INTERVIEW SKILLS
>
> Verifying Information
> Reporting Personal Information
> Correcting

NEW VOCABULARY

at	new
current	no
it	still
live	

GETTING READY

Introduce Yes/No questions and short answers.

a. Write on the board:

> | | |
> |---|---|
> | Are you from Mexico? | Yes, I am. |
> | | No, I'm not. |

b. Ask the question and model the answer for each student. Then ask each student the question, and have him/her respond appropriately.

c. Write on the board:

> | | |
> |---|---|
> | Is your name Maria? | Yes, it is. |
> | | No, it isn't. |

d. Ask the question and model the answer for each student. Then ask each student the question and have him/her respond appropriately.

PRACTICING THE MODEL DIALOGS

For each dialog:

1. **Setting the Scene:** Have students look at the photograph and determine who is talking: an INS examiner and an applicant. Establish the context: "The INS examiner is asking about the applicant's address."

2. **Listening:** With books closed, have students listen to the dialog—presented by you, by a pair of students, or on the audio program.

3. **Choral Repetition:** With books still closed, model each line and have the whole class repeat in unison.

4. **Reading:** With books open, have students follow along as two students present the model dialog. Ask students if they have any questions and check understanding of vocabulary.

5. **Choral Conversation Practice:** Divide the class in half. Have Group 1 ask the questions and Group 2 give the answers; then reverse. (Or: You ask the questions and have the whole class answer in unison; then reverse.)

6. Call on one or two pairs of students to present the model dialog.

PRACTICING NEW DIALOGS

1. Call on one or two pairs of students to present new dialogs, using one of the skeletal dialogs as a guide and filling in the blanks with the appropriate information.

2. **Pair Practice:** Have students practice making new dialogs in pairs, taking turns being the INS examiner and the applicant.

3. Call on one or two more pairs of students to present their new dialogs to the class.

GRAMMAR CHECK

1. I am	3. I'm not
2. it is	4. it isn't

TEXT PAGES 28–29: INTERVIEW: *Let Me Verify Some Information*

FOCUS

TOPICS

Personal Information
Dates

GRAMMAR

Yes/No Questions

Is your date of birth November 20, 1968?
Is that correct?

Short Answers

Yes, it is.
No, it isn't.

WH-Questions

What's your social security number?

FUNCTIONAL INTERVIEW SKILLS

Verifying Information
Correcting

NEW VOCABULARY

correct	All right.
some	I see.
verify	Let me. . .

PRACTICING THE MODEL DIALOG

1. **Setting the Scene:** Have students look at the photograph and determine who is talking: an INS examiner and an applicant. Establish the context: "The INS examiner is asking the applicant some personal information."

2. **Listening:** With books closed, have students listen to the dialog—presented by you, by a pair of students, or on the audio program.

3. **Choral Repetition:** With books still closed, model each line and have the whole class repeat in unison.

4. **Reading:** With books open, have students follow along as two students present the model dialog. Ask students if they have any questions and check understanding of vocabulary.

5. **Choral Conversation Practice:** Divide the class in half. Have Group 1 ask the questions and Group 2 give the answers; then reverse. (Or: You ask the questions and have the whole class answer in unison; then reverse.)

6. Call on one or two pairs of students to present the model dialog.

PRACTICING NEW DIALOGS

1. Call on one or two pairs of students to present new dialogs, using the skeletal dialog as a guide and filling in the blanks with the appropriate information.

2. **Pair Practice:** Have students practice making new dialogs in pairs, taking turns being the INS examiner and the applicant.

3. Call on one or two more pairs of students to present their new dialogs to the class.

FILL OUT THE FORM

Have students fill out the form with their personal information. Low-beginning-level students may need to copy the information from a model. Make sure students write in capital letters.

TEXT PAGE 30: *Check-Up*

QUESTIONS AND ANSWERS

This exercise offers students important practice with the multiple ways a question might be posed by the INS examiner. First, have students repeat each question after you. Then, have students practice asking and answering the questions with other students. Finally, have students write their answers to questions 1, 2, and 3.

LISTENING

In order to do the listening exercises, students will first need to write their place of birth on line A and date of birth on line B. Low-beginning-level students may have to copy this information from a model.

Have students complete the exercises as you play the audio program or read the following:

Listen carefully and circle A or B.

1. Where were you born?
2. What's your date of birth?
3. What's your place of birth?
4. When were you born?
5. Where are you from?
6. What's your birth date?

Answers

1. A	4. B
2. B	5. A
3. A	6. B

TEXT PAGE 31: *Information Exchange*

Have the entire class practice asking the questions in the box at the top of the page. Then have students circulate around the room and interview six other students, writing the information they gather in the appropriate place on the grid. (For additional speaking practice, students can later report back to the class and tell about the students they interviewed.)

ADDITIONAL PRACTICE

Have students work in pairs, taking turns asking and answering the nine questions. (For additional practice, students can write the answers to the questions on a separate sheet of paper.)

TEXT PAGES 32–33: *Chapter Test*

You can use this test as a standardized form of assessment to measure student achievement of the curriculum objectives in Chapter B. The test consists of 20 multiple-choice items and five sentences for dictation.

To score the test on a scale of 100:

- For each correct multiple-choice item, score four points.

- For each dictation sentence, do a general evaluation of the correctness of words, spelling, punctuation, and legibility. Score each sentence as follows:

  4 (Excellent), **3** (Good), **2** (Fair), **1** (Poor), **0** (Unsatisfactory)

Students can write their answers in the text or on the reproducible Chapter Test Answer Sheet provided in the Appendix.

A. PERSONAL INFORMATION

1. B
2. B
3. C
4. A
5. D
6. C
7. D
8. A
9. D
10. C
11. C
12. B

B. VOCABULARY

13. A
14. B
15. D
16. A
17. C
18. D
19. C
20. B

C. DICTATION

Have students write these sentences as you read each sentence twice or play the audio program:

1. I am from _____.
   (name of country)
2. My home is in _____.
   (name of city or town)
3. I am living in the United States of America.
4. This is my telephone number.
5. I want to be a citizen of the United States.

TEXT PAGE 34: *Civics Enrichment*

PERFORMANCE-BASED ASSESSMENT

These civics enrichment activities are designed to promote students' active participation in class and in the civic life of the community—through projects, issues discussions, community tasks, field trips, and Internet activities. Reproducible performance-based assessment forms for use in evaluating and documenting student participation in these activities are included in the Appendix.

CIVIC PARTICIPATION

First have students practice introducing themselves in class. Then have them go around the school and introduce themselves to various school personnel in the office, in the library, or other places. They should tell their name, their nationality, where they were born, when they came to the United States, and other information they would like to share.

PROJECT ACTIVITY

Bulletin Board Project: In this project, students first work individually. They bring in a map of their native country (a real map or one they have drawn), and they write a paragraph about themselves. In the paragraph, they tell their name, nationality, country of birth, and the city or town where they were born. Then students work as a class to make a bulletin board display of their work. Have students take responsibility for all aspects of this project. Have them identify the particular tasks involved in the project, who will accomplish each task, what resources are needed, and what form the final bulletin board display will take. Use the project as a basis for building students' skills in leadership, teamwork, and communicating information—key SCANS* skills useful for success in the workplace.

*Secretary's Commission on Achieving Necessary Skills.

PROJECT ACTIVITY

Calendar Project: In this project students work as a class to make a calendar with separate pages for each month that they will study together in your class. On the calendar they should indicate their birthdays, U.S. holidays, native country holidays, and other special dates. Have students take responsibility for all aspects of this project. Have them identify the particular tasks involved in the project, who will accomplish each task, what resources are needed, and what form the final calendar will take. Use the project as a basis for building students' leadership and teamwork skills.

| CHAPTER 1 | OVERVIEW Student Text Pages 35–48 |

TOPICS

Maps & Geography
Cities, States, & Capitals
Beliefs

GRAMMAR

Simple Present Tense
Simple Present Tense vs. To Be
WH-Questions
Yes/No Questions
Short Answers

FUNCTIONAL INTERVIEW SKILLS

Reporting Information
Expressing Beliefs

KEY VOCABULARY

GEOGRAPHY
Atlantic Ocean
Austin
Canada
capital
Chicago
city
country
Dallas
Illinois
map
Mexico
ocean
Pacific Ocean
state
state capital
Texas
town
the United States of America
Washington, D.C.

COMPASS DIRECTIONS
east
north
south
west

PERSONAL INFORMATION
family members
name
native country

OTHER VOCABULARY
apply
believe
between
big
citizen
Communism
Communist Party
Constitution
democracy
enter
freedom
friends
government
large
live
member

name (v.)
naturalization
other
party
permanent
  resident
point
some day
terrorist
  organization
totalitarian
visit
want to
what
where
which

RELATED PRACTICE

Foundations: Chapter 2
Word by Word Basic: pages 8–11, 167–171
Word by Word: pages 4–9
Side by Side Book 1: Chapters 9, 10
Side by Side Interactive CD-ROM / Side by Side TV Video: Level 1A, Segment 13;
    Level 1B, Segments 14, 15
ExpressWays Book 1: Chapter 2

TEXT PAGE 35: *Vocabulary Preview*

You may want to introduce these words before beginning the chapter, or you may choose to wait until they first occur in a specific lesson. If you choose to introduce them at this point, here are some suggestions:

1. Have students look at the map on text page 35 and identify the words they already know.

2. Present the vocabulary. Say each word and have the class repeat it chorally and individually. Check students' understanding and pronunciation of the words.

3. Practice the vocabulary as a class, in pairs, or in small groups. Have students cover the word list and look at the map. Practice the words in the following ways:
   - Say a word and have students tell the number of the word on the map.
   - Give the number of something on the map and have students say the word.

TEXT PAGES 36–37: *A Map of the United States of America*

FOCUS

TOPIC

Maps & Geography
Cities, States, & Capitals

GRAMMAR

To Be (Review)

The United States **is** a large country.
Canada **is** north of the United States.

WH-Questions

What's the name of your state?

NEW VOCABULARY

Atlantic Ocean	our
between	Pacific Ocean
Canada	Washington, D.C.
capital	north
large	south
map	east
ocean	west
other	

GETTING READY

Introduce directions.

    a. Use the map on page 36. Point to the top of the map and say, "This is north." Repeat for south, east, and west.

    b. Have students identify the direction as you point north, south, east, and west in random order several times.

PREVIEWING THE STORY

Have students talk about the map to establish the context of the story. Ask some or all of the following questions:

What country is this?
How many states are there in the United States?
Where is Texas?/ Point to Texas.
Where is California?/ Point to California.
Where is Florida?/ Point to Florida.
Where is New York?/ Point to New York.
Where is our state?/ Point to our state.
What state is north of *(your state)*?
What state is south of *(your state)*?
What state is east of *(your state)*?
What state is west of *(your state)*?

READING THE STORY

1. Have students read the story silently.

2. **Check Reading Comprehension**: Ask students a question about each line of the story. For beginning-level students, ask these questions in the order below so that the questions follow the sequence of the story. For higher-level students, ask the questions in random order.

   What is this?
   What country is this a map of?

   Is the United States a large country or a small country?
   What countries is the United States between?
   Where is Canada?/ What country is north of the United States?
   Where is Mexico?/ What country is south of the United States?

   Is the United States between two oceans?
   What ocean is east of the United States?
   What ocean is west of the United States?

   What is the capital of the United States?

3. Ask students if they have any questions about the story; check understanding of vocabulary.

4. **Choral Repetition**: Read aloud each line of the story and have students repeat.

5. **Class Circle Reading:** Have students read the story aloud as a class, with different students reading each line. (You can assign each line to a particular student or by seating patterns, or by letting students take turns spontaneously. In large classes, have a different group or row of students read each line.)

6. **Pair Practice:** Have students work in pairs, reading the passage to each other paragraph by paragraph. Circulate around the room and check students' reading and pronunciation, focusing more attention on students who need more assistance.

EXPANSION

1. *Map Reading*

Bring in a map of the United States (or use the one on page 36). Point to different states and have students identify which states are north, south, east, and west of the state you pointed to. Ask individual students to point to states and have the rest of the class identify which states are north, south, east, and west of that state.

2. *Personal Information on the Map*

Using the map on page 36 or another map you bring in, have students point to states that are important in their lives and tell why, such as states where relatives live, states where students have previously lived, etc.

VOCABULARY CHECK

1. country
2. north
3. capital
4. east
5. west
6. south

GRAMMAR CHECK

1. Yes, it is.
2. No, it isn't.
3. Yes, it is.
4. No, it isn't.
5. Yes, it is.
6. Yes, it is.

MAP GAME

Students can look at the map on page 36 or a classroom map as they play this game. For a more challenging game, don't allow students to refer to a map as they play.

TEXT PAGE 39: *Your Native Country*

First, have students draw a map of their country in their books. Students should indicate the location of their country's capital, their city or town, and the countries or bodies of water that are next to their countries.

Then, have students answer the questions about their countries. (Low-beginning-level students may need help providing this information.)

FOCUS

> ### TOPIC
>
> Cities, States, and Capitals
>
> ### GRAMMAR
>
> **Simple Present Tense**
>
> I **live** in Texas.
>
> **WH-Questions**
>
> **What** state do you live in?
>
> ### FUNCTIONAL INTERVIEW SKILL
>
> Reporting Information

NEW VOCABULARY

> name (v.)

GETTING READY

Introduce the simple present tense.

    a. Write on the board:

> What state do you live in?
> I live in *(your state).*

    b. Ask the question and model the answer.

    c. Ask each student the question and have him/her respond appropriately.

PRACTICING THE MODEL DIALOG

1. **Setting the Scene:** Have students look at the photograph and determine who is talking: an INS examiner and an applicant. Establish the context: "The INS examiner is asking questions about where the applicant lives."

2. **Listening:** With books closed, have students listen to the dialog—presented by you, by a pair of students, or on the audio program.

3. **Choral Repetition:** With books still closed, model each line and have the whole class repeat in unison.

4. **Reading:** With books open, have students follow along as two students present the model dialog. Ask students if they have any questions and check understanding of vocabulary.

5. **Choral Conversation Practice:** Divide the class in half. Have Group 1 ask the questions and Group 2 give the answers; then reverse. (Or: You ask the questions and have the whole class answer in unison; then reverse.)

6. Call on one or two pairs of students to present the model dialog.

PRACTICING NEW DIALOGS

1. Call on one or two pairs of students to present new dialogs, using the skeletal dialog as a guide and filling in the blanks with the appropriate information.

2. **Pair Practice:** Have students practice making new dialogs in pairs, taking turns being the INS examiner and the applicant.

3. Call on one or two more pairs of students to present their new dialogs to the class.

TEXT PAGE 41: *Check-Up*

GETTING READY

Contrast the verb *to be* and the simple present tense.

Write on the board:

> What's the name of your state?
> The name of my state is *(your state)*.
>
> What state do you live in?
> I live in *(your state)*.

Say the sentences and have students repeat them chorally and individually.

QUESTIONS AND ANSWERS

This exercise offers students important practice with the multiple ways a question might be posed by the INS examiner. First, have students repeat each question after you. Then, have students practice asking and answering the questions with other students. Finally, have students write their answers to questions 1, 2, 3, and 4.

LISTENING

In order to do the listening exercises, students will first need to write the name of their state on line A, the name of their state capital on line B, and *Washington, D.C.* on line C. Low-beginning-level students may have to copy this information from a model.

Have students complete the exercises as you play the audio program or read the following:

> *Listen and circle A, B, or C.*
>
> 1. What's the name of your state?
> 2. Name the capital of the United States.
> 3. What's the name of your state capital?
> 4. What state do you live in?
> 5. Name the capital of your state.
> 6. What's the capital of the United States?
>
> **Answers**
>
> | | |
> |---|---|
> | 1. A | 4. A |
> | 2. C | 5. B |
> | 3. B | 6. C |

TEXT PAGE 42: *I Believe in the United States*

FOCUS

> ### TOPIC
> Beliefs
>
> ### GRAMMAR
>
> **Simple Present Tense**
>
> I **believe** in the United States.
> I **don't believe** in Communism.
>
> **Simple Present Tense vs. To Be**
>
> I **live** in Chicago.
> Chicago **is** a big city in Illinois.
>
> I **don't believe** in Communism.
> I **am not** a member of the Communist Party.
>
> ### FUNCTIONAL INTERVIEW SKILL
>
> Expressing Beliefs

NEW VOCABULARY

> | | | |
> |---|---|---|
> | believe | democracy | terrorist |
> | big | freedom | organization |
> | citizen | government | totalitarian |
> | Communism | member | party |
> | Communist Party | naturalization | want |
> | Constitution | | |

PREVIEWING THE STORY

Have students talk about the story title and the photograph to establish the context of the story. Ask some or all of the following questions:

> What's he doing? / What's his job?
> What does he believe in?
> What is Communism?
> Is the United States a communist country?

READING THE STORY

1. Have students read the story silently.

2. **Check Reading Comprehension:** Ask students a question about each line of the story. For beginning-level students, ask these questions in the order below so that the questions follow the sequence of the story. For higher-level students, ask the questions in random order.

   What's his name?
   Where does he live?
   Where is Chicago? / Is Chicago large or small?

   What country does he believe in?
   What government does he believe in?
   What constitution does he believe in?
   Does he believe in Communism?

   Is he a member of the Communist Party?
   Is he a member of any other totalitarian party?
   Is he a member of any terrorist organization?

   What else does he believe in?
   What is he applying for?
   What does he want to be?

3. Ask students if they have any questions about the story; check understanding of vocabulary.

4. **Choral Repetition:** Read aloud each line of the story and have students repeat.

5. **Class Circle Reading:** Have students read the story aloud as a class, with different students reading each line. (You can assign each line to a particular student or by seating patterns, or by letting students take turns spontaneously. In large classes, have a different group or row of students read each line.)

6. **Pair Practice:** Have students work in pairs, reading the passage to each other paragraph by paragraph. Circulate around the room and check students' reading and pronunciation, focusing more attention on students who need more assistance.

DID YOU UNDERSTAND?

Have students answer these questions in complete sentences.

1. His name is Stanislaw Bienkowski.
2. He lives in Chicago.
3. No, he doesn't.
4. He believes in the United States.
5. He wants to be a citizen of the United States.

VOCABULARY CHECK

1. city
2. democracy
3. citizen
4. naturalization
5. capital
6. state

DISCUSSION

Lead a class discussion about freedom and democracy based on these questions.

GRAMMAR CHECK

Have students answer these questions as they would at an INS interview. (Although questions about political beliefs are not officially included in the 100 questions the INS uses to test English and Civics knowledge, such questions have been asked during naturalization interviews.)

1. Yes, I do.
2. No, I don't.
3. Yes, I do.
4. Yes, I do.
5. No, I don't. ("Yes, I do" for residents of Chicago.)
6. Yes, I do.
7. Yes, I am. (for permanent residents)
8. No, I'm not. (for non-citizens)
9. No, I don't. ("Yes, I do" for residents of Washington, D.C.)
10. No, I'm not.
11. Yes, I do.
12. Yes, I am.

REVIEW

Have the class work in pairs, taking turns asking and answering the questions. For additional practice, students can write the answers to these questions on a separate sheet of paper.

TEXT PAGE 45: SONG OF FREEDOM: *America the Beautiful*

PRACTICING THE SONG

1. **Listening to the Lyrics:** Have students listen to the lyrics of the song by playing the audio or saying the lyrics yourself.

2. **Choral Repetition:** Read aloud each line of the song and have students repeat in unison.

3. **Listening to the Song:** Have students listen to the song by playing the audio or singing it yourself.

4. **Singing Aloud:** Play the instrumental version of the song and have students sing along. (The instrumental version follows the vocal version on the audio program.)

EXPANSION

Discuss with students the photo of Pike's Peak and the information in the caption.

You can use this test as a standardized form of assessment to measure student achievement of the curriculum objectives in Chapter 1. The test consists of 20 multiple-choice items and five sentences for dictation.

To score the test on a scale of 100:

- For each correct multiple-choice item, score four points.

- For each dictation sentence, do a general evaluation of the correctness of words, spelling, punctuation, and legibility. Score each sentence as follows:

    4 (Excellent), **3** (Good), **2** (Fair), **1** (Poor), **0** (Unsatisfactory)

Students can write their answers in the text or on the reproducible Chapter Test Answer Sheet provided in the Appendix.

A. CITIES, STATES, CAPITALS, & GEOGRAPHY

1. C
2. D
3. A
4. B
5. D
6. D
7. C
8. D
9. B
10. D
11. A
12. C

B. GRAMMAR & VOCABULARY

13. D
14. B
15. C
16. C
17. B
18. A
19. C
20. A

C. DICTATION

Have students write these sentences as you read each sentence twice or play the audio program:

1. The United States is a large country.
2. I live in a big city.
3. The capital of the United States is Washington, D.C.
4. I believe in the Constitution of the United States.
5. Texas is a large state.

PERFORMANCE-BASED ASSESSMENT

These civics enrichment activities are designed to promote students' active participation in class and in the civic life of the community – through projects, issues discussions, community tasks, field trips, and Internet activities. Reproducible performance-based assessment forms for use in evaluating and documenting student participation in these activities are included in the Appendix.

CIVIC PARTICIPATION

For this activity, bring to class one or more local street maps of your community. (If possible, bring in a sufficient number of maps so that students can work in pairs or in small groups.) Have students identify the kind of information they see on the map. Have them find the location of their school on the map. Then have them find the locations where they live. Have students bring in other kinds of maps of the community, such as bus route maps, subway maps, and maps of parks, bicycle routes, or other local features. (Brainstorm with students where they can find these maps, and then have students obtain them. While it may seem easier for you to supply them, a key goal of the activity is for students to access community resources such as the library, city hall, or parks and recreation department in order to locate the materials.) When students have brought in the maps, have a class discussion about the kinds of information the maps provide.

PROJECT ACTIVITY

In this project, students work as a class to make a big tourist map for visitors to your community. Students should draw all the important places to visit and show where they are located. They should try to show all the important streets and also show any bus or train routes tourists can use to visit the places on the map. (You can use a tourist map of another city as an example. Don't use a tourist map of your own city as students might replicate it.) Have students take responsibility for all aspects of this project. Have them identify the particular tasks involved in the project, who will accomplish each task, what resources are needed, and what form the final tourist map will take. Use the project as a basis for building students' skills in leadership, teamwork, and communicating information—key SCANS* skills useful for success in the workplace.

*Secretary's Commission on Achieving Necessary Skills.

COMMUNITY ISSUES

Problem-Posing Discussion: Have students discuss whether their neighborhood and their school are in good locations or bad locations. Have them identify any problems with transportation from their neighborhood to their school and to other important places in the community. Encourage students to explore the issue of equity in transportation services in your community. Do some neighborhoods have better transportation services than others? What are the reasons? As students identify key issues and problems, have them share ideas about how to solve them. How might students request better bus routes, new bus stops, expanded subway or light-rail services, or other transportation improvements?

TECHNOLOGY ENRICHMENT

See Appendix page 159 for Internet enrichment activities related to this chapter.

<table>
<tr>
<td>

CHAPTER 2

</td>
<td>

OVERVIEW
Student Text
Pages 49–58

</td>
</tr>
</table>

TOPIC

The Flag

GRAMMAR

There Is/There Are
Singular/Plural
Have/Has

FUNCTIONAL INTERVIEW SKILLS

Reporting Information
Asking for Repetition
Hesitating

KEY VOCABULARY

THE FLAG
American flag
flag
star
stripe
U.S. flag

COLORS
blue
brown
red
white

PLACES
island
Iwo Jima
moon
mountain
Mount Suribachi
United States
World Trade Center

PEOPLE
astronaut
firefighter
U.S. Marines

EVENTS
battle
terrorist attack
World War II

OTHER WORDS
colonies
native country
plant (v.)
raise (v.)
site
states
top

FUNCTIONAL EXPRESSIONS
Certainly.
Could you please repeat the question?
That's right.
Uh . . . let me see.

RELATED PRACTICE

Foundations: Chapters 3, 9
Word by Word Basic: pages 12–17, 98–109
Word by Word: pages 10–11, 56–61
Side by Side Book 1: Chapters 7, 8
Side by Side Interactive CD-ROM / Side by Side TV Video: Level 1A, Segments 9–12
ExpressWays Book 1: Chapter 4

You may want to introduce these words before beginning the chapter, or you may choose to wait until they first occur in a specific lesson. If you choose to introduce them at this point, here are some suggestions:

1. Have students look at the photographs on text page 49 and identify the words they already know.

2. Present the vocabulary. Say each word and have the class repeat it chorally and individually. Check students' understanding and pronunciation of the words.

3. Practice the vocabulary as a class, in pairs, or in small groups. Have students cover the word list and look at the photographs. Practice the words in the following ways:

   • Say a word and have students tell the correct number on the photograph.
   • Give a number on a photograph and have students say the word.

TEXT PAGE 50: *The Flag of the United States*

FOCUS

TOPIC

The Flag

GRAMMAR

There Is / There Are

There is one star for each state.
There are fifty stars on the American flag.

Singular/Plural

There is one stripe for each of the first thirteen states.
There are thirteen stripes on the American flag.

NEW VOCABULARY

American	fifty	star
blue	flag	stripe
call	one	there
colony	red	thirteen
color	seven	three
each	six	white

GETTING READY

1. Introduce singular and plural.

   Give examples of singular and plural nouns by pointing out objects in the room. For example:

   a book—books
   a window—windows

2. Introduce *there is/there are.*

   Using the singular and plural nouns from the first Getting Ready activity, make sentences using *there is* or *there are.* For example: "There is one book on the desk." "There are ten books on the shelf."

3. Introduce colors.

   Use colored paper or objects in the room to introduce the colors red, white, and blue.

   a. Show students the red paper or object and say "Red." Have students repeat. Continue for white and blue.
   b. Ask about the color of objects or articles of clothing in the room that are red, white, or blue. For example, point to a student and ask, "What color is his shirt?" ("White.")

PREVIEWING THE STORY

Have students talk about the story title and the photograph to establish the context of the story. Ask some or all of the following questions:

What is this?
Where do you see it? (School? Community? Sporting events? TV?)
What are the colors of the American flag?
What is on the American flag?

READING THE STORY

1. Have students read the story silently.

2. **Check Reading Comprehension:** Ask students a question about each line of the story. For beginning-level students, ask these questions in the order below so that the questions follow the sequence of the story. For higher-level students, ask the questions in random order.

> How many colors are there on the flag of the United States?
>
> What color is the American flag?
>
> How many states are there in the United States?
>
> How many stars are there on the American flag?
>
> How many stars are there for each state?
>
> How many stripes are there on the American flag?
>
> What colors are the stripes?
>
> How many red stripes are there? How many white stripes are there?
>
> Why are there thirteen stripes on the flag?
>
> What were the first thirteen states called?

3. Ask students if they have any questions about the story; check understanding of vocabulary.

4. **Choral Repetition:** Read aloud each line of the story and have students repeat.

5. **Class Circle Reading:** Have students read the story aloud as a class, with different students reading each line. (You can assign each line to a particular student or by seating patterns, or by letting students take turns spontaneously. In large classes, have a different group or row of students read each line.)

6. **Pair Practice:** Have students work in pairs, reading the passage to each other paragraph by paragraph. Circulate around the room and check students' reading and pronunciation, focusing more attention on students who need more assistance.

EXPANSION

1. Have students orally describe the flags of their countries. Teach the names of additional colors, shapes, animals, and other symbols on these flags.

2. Have students practice *there is / there are* as they describe objects in the classroom and locations around the school. For example:

> There is a pencil on my desk.
> There are books on the shelf.
> There is a post office next to our school.

TEXT PAGES 51–52: *Check-Up*

DID YOU UNDERSTAND?

1. The American flag is red, white, and blue. OR, The colors of the American flag are red, white, and blue.
2. There are fifty states in the United States.
3. There are fifty stars on the American flag.
4. There are thirteen stripes on the flag.
5. The stripes are red and white.

VOCABULARY CHECK

1. blue
2. stripes
3. stars
4. colors
5. red
6. colonies

GRAMMAR CHECK

1. There are
2. There is
3. There are
4. There are
5. There is
6. There are

YOUR NATIVE COUNTRY'S FLAG

Have each student draw his or her native country's flag. (If possible, have crayons available so that students can depict the flags' colors. If not, ask students to color the flags at home.)

Have students write answers to the questions about their flags, and then share this information with other students.

How Many Stars Does the American Flag Have?

FOCUS

TOPIC

The Flag

GRAMMAR

Have / Has

How many stars does the American flag **have**?
It **has** fifty stars.

FUNCTIONAL INTERVIEW SKILLS

Reporting Information
Asking for Repetition
Hesitating

NEW VOCABULARY

certainly	question
has	repeat
how many	

GETTING READY

Introduce *have/has*.

a. Write on the board:

> How many stars does the American
>   flag have?
> It has fifty stars.

b. Model the question and answer for the students, and have them repeat chorally and individually.

c. Continue with the same question about stripes and colors.

d. Ask students other questions, such as:

How many pages does our book have?
How many windows does our classroom have?
How many rooms does your apartment have?

PRACTICING THE MODEL DIALOG

1. **Setting the Scene:** Have students look at the photograph and determine the subject of the conversation: "The INS examiner is asking questions about the American flag."

2. **Listening:** With books closed, have students listen to the dialog—presented by you, by a pair of students, or on the audio program.

3. **Choral Repetition:** With books still closed, model each line and have the whole class repeat in unison.

4. **Reading:** With books open, have students follow along as two students present the model dialog. Ask students if they have any questions and check understanding of vocabulary.

5. **Choral Conversation Practice:** Divide the class in half. Have Group 1 ask the questions and Group 2 give the answers; then reverse. (Or: You ask the questions and have the whole class answer in unison; then reverse.)

6. Call on one or two pairs of students to present the model dialog.

PRACTICING NEW DIALOGS

1. Call on one or two pairs of students to present new dialogs, using the skeletal dialog as a guide and filling in the blanks with the appropriate information.

2. **Pair Practice:** Have students practice making new dialogs in pairs, taking turns being the INS examiner and the applicant.

3. Call on one or two more pairs of students to present their new dialogs to the class.

> 1. A. How many *stripes* does the American flag have?
>   B. I'm sorry. Could you please repeat the question?
>   A. Certainly. How many *stripes* does the American flag have?
>   B. Uh . . . let me see. It has *thirteen stripes*.
>   A. That's right.

2. A. How many *colors* does the American
      flag have?
   B. I'm sorry. Could you please repeat
      the question?
   A. Certainly. How many *colors* does the
      American flag have?
   B. Uh . . . let me see. It has *three colors*.
   A. That's right.

TEXT PAGE 54: *Check-Up*

QUESTIONS AND ANSWERS

This exercise offers students important practice with
the multiple ways a question might be posed by the
INS examiner. First, have students repeat each
question after you. Then, have students practice
asking and answering the questions with other
students. Finally, have students write their answers
to questions 1–4.

1. The American flag has thirteen stripes.
2. There are thirteen stripes on the
   American flag.
3. The American flag has fifty stars.
4. There are fifty states in the United States.

LISTENING

Have students complete the exercises as you play
the audio program or read the following:

Listen and circle the correct answer.

1. How many states are there in the United
   States?
2. How many stripes does the American
   flag have?
3. How many colors does the American
   flag have?
4. What were the first thirteen states called?
5. What are the colors of the American flag?
6. What colors are the stripes on the flag of
   the United States?

Answers

1. 50	3. 3	5. red, white, and blue
2. 13	4. colonies	6. red and white

TEXT PAGE 55: *The Pledge of Allegiance*

PRACTICING THE PLEDGE OF ALLEGIANCE

*(Note: You may want to have students stand and
place their right hands on their chests while
practicing the Pledge in parts or in its entirety.)*

1. **Choral Repetition (line by line):** Read aloud
   each line and have students repeat in unison.

2. **Choral Repetition (phrase by phrase):** Read
   aloud each phrase and have students repeat in
   unison, as follows:

I pledge allegiance to the flag of the United
   States of America /

and to the republic for which it stands, /

one nation, under God, indivisible, /

with liberty and justice for all.

3. **Reading:** Have students practice reading the
   Pledge as a class, in small groups, or on their
   own.

4. **Reciting:** Have students memorize the Pledge
   and practice reciting it as a class, in small
   groups, and on their own.

EXPANSION

1. Discuss with students the photos and information in the captions:

   PHOTO 1: Astronauts Neil Armstrong and Buzz Aldrin planting the U.S. flag on the moon on July 20, 1969.

   PHOTO 2: U.S. Marines raising the U.S. flag on Iwo Jima during World War II. Tell students about the Marine memorial in the nation's capital that depicts this scene, and bring in a photo of the memorial if available.

PHOTO 3: Firefighters raising the flag at the site of the World Trade Center in New York City after the terrorist attack on September 11, 2001. Ask students what they remember about that day, and have them discuss their thoughts and feelings about the events.

2. Tell students about when *you* say/said the Pledge of Allegiance: as a child (school? scout troop?) and as an adult (meetings? assemblies?).

3. Ask students to recite pledges of their native countries in their native languages and then explain in English what they mean.

TEXT PAGES 56–57: *Chapter Test*

You can use this test as a standardized form of assessment to measure student achievement of the curriculum objectives in Chapter 2. The test consists of 20 multiple-choice items and five sentences for dictation.

To score the test on a scale of 100:

- For each correct multiple-choice item, score four points.

- For each dictation sentence, do a general evaluation of the correctness of words, spelling, punctuation, and legibility. Score each sentence as follows:

   4 (Excellent), **3** (Good), **2** (Fair), **1** (Poor), **0** (Unsatisfactory)

Students can write their answers in the text or on the reproducible Chapter Test Answer Sheet provided in the Appendix.

A. THE FLAG

1. D
2. C
3. C
4. A
5. B
6. C
7. D
8. D
9. B
10. C
11. B
12. B

B. GRAMMAR & VOCABULARY

13. C
14. A
15. A
16. B
17. C
18. D
19. B
20. D

C. DICTATION

Have students write these sentences as you read each sentence twice or play the audio program:

1. There are fifty (50) states in the United States.
2. The American flag has three (3) colors.
3. The flag is red, white, and blue.
4. The flag of the United States has thirteen (13) stripes.
5. There are fifty (50) stars on the flag.

PERFORMANCE-BASED ASSESSMENT

These civics enrichment activities are designed to promote students' active participation in class and in the civic life of the community—through projects, issues discussions, community tasks, field trips, and Internet activities. Reproducible performance-based assessment forms for use in evaluating and documenting student participation in these activities are included in the Appendix.

CIVIC PARTICIPATION

Discussion: Have students discuss where they see the flag of the United States in your community and what other kinds of flags they see. Then have them discuss the symbols and colors on your state flag.

PROJECT ACTIVITY

Bulletin Board "Flags of the World" Project: In this project, students draw color pictures of the flags of their native countries, they write some sentences that describe the flags, and then they work as a class to make a bulletin board display containing their drawings, their sentences, and perhaps their photographs labeled with their names and native countries. Have students take responsibility for all aspects of this project. Have them identify the particular tasks involved in the project, who will accomplish each task, what resources are needed, and what form the final bulletin board display will take. Use the project as a basis for building students' skills in leadership, teamwork, and communicating information—key SCANS* skills useful for success in the workplace. (If possible, use a bulletin board in the school cafeteria, near the main office, or in another highly visible location so that the display is seen by the greatest number of people.)

*Secretary's Commission on Achieving Necessary Skills

INTERNET ACTIVITY

In this activity, students use an Internet search engine to find information to answer questions about the flag. This activity enables students to develop basic computer skills, such as using a computer keyboard and mouse, and to perform such tasks as clicking, scrolling, dragging, keyboarding, using an Internet browser, typing search words to find information, and typing URLs to access websites. Make sure students have the skills to access the Internet and to use the computer to search for the information about the flag. Students can use **www.yahoo.com**, **www.google.com**, or another search engine for this activity.

Answers to the questions are as follows:

- The flag flies at half-mast when public officials request it after someone in the government dies.

- If you want to fly the flag at night, you must have a light shine on it.

- The flag flies in front of the White House only when the President is staying there.

TECHNOLOGY ENRICHMENT

See Appendix page 159 for additional Internet enrichment activities related to this chapter.

<table>
<tr><td>

CHAPTER 3

</td><td>

OVERVIEW
Student Text
Pages 59–70

</td></tr>
</table>

TOPIC

Branches of Government

GRAMMAR

Simple Present Tense
Have/Has
Can

FUNCTIONAL INTERVIEW SKILLS

Reporting Information
Checking Understanding
Hesitating

KEY VOCABULARY

BRANCHES OF GOVERNMENT

executive
judicial
legislative

PEOPLE

Congress
President
representative
senator
Supreme Court justice
Vice President

BUILDINGS & PLACES

Capitol
Supreme Court
Washington, D.C.
White House

QUESTION WORDS

how many
what
where
which
who

OTHER WORDS

called
can
enforce the laws
explain the laws
have – has
laws
live
make the laws
work

FUNCTIONAL EXPRESSIONS

Can you tell me . . . ?
Hmm.
I think . . .
Name . . .
That's correct.
That's right.
Very good.

RELATED PRACTICE

Foundations: Chapter 4
Word by Word Basic: pages 18–29, 40–45
Word by Word: pages 13–18, 25–27
Side by Side Book 1: Chapter 11
Side by Side Interactive CD-ROM / Side by Side TV Video: Level 1B, Segments 16, 17
ExpressWays Book 1: Chapter 3

TEXT PAGE 59: *Vocabulary Preview*

You may want to introduce these words before beginning the chapter, or you may choose to wait until they first occur in a specific lesson. If you choose to introduce them at this point, here are some suggestions:

1. Have students look at the photographs on text page 59 and identify the words they already know.

2. Present the vocabulary. Say each word and have the class repeat it chorally and individually. Check students' understanding and pronunciation of the words.

3. Practice the vocabulary as a class, in pairs, or in small groups. Have students cover the word list and look at the photographs. Practice the words in the following ways:

   • Say a word and have students tell the number of the photograph.
   • Give the number of a photograph and have students say the word.

TEXT PAGE 60: *Branches of Government*

FOCUS

TOPIC

Branches of Government

GRAMMAR

Simple Present Tense

Senators and representatives **work** in the legislative branch.

Have/Has

The government of the United States **has** three parts.

NEW VOCABULARY

branch	representative
executive branch	senator
judicial branch	Supreme Court
legislative branch	Supreme Court justice
part	Vice President
President	

PREVIEWING THE STORY

Have students talk about the story title and the photographs to establish the context of the story. Ask some or all of the following questions:

(Point to the first picture.)
What is this?
Where is this?
Who works there?

(Point to the second picture.)
What is this?
Where is this?
Who works there?
Who lives there?

(Point to the third picture.)
What is this?
Where is this?
Who works there?

READING THE STORY

1. Have students read the story silently.
2. **Check Reading Comprehension:** Ask students a question about each line of the story. For beginning-level students, ask these questions in the order below so that the questions follow the sequence of the story. For higher-level students, ask the questions in random order.

   How many parts does the government of the United States have? What are the three parts called?

What are the names of the three branches of government?

Who works in the legislative branch?
Who works in the executive branch?
Who works in the judicial branch?

3. Ask students if they have any questions about the story; check understanding of vocabulary.
4. **Choral Repetition:** Read aloud each line of the story and have students repeat.
5. **Class Circle Reading:** Have students read the story aloud as a class, with different students reading each line. (You can assign each line to a particular student or by seating patterns, or by letting students take turns spontaneously. In large classes, have a different group or row of students read each line.)
6. **Pair Practice:** Have students work in pairs, reading the passage to each other paragraph by paragraph. Circulate around the room and check students' reading and pronunciation, focusing more attention on students who need more assistance.

TEXT PAGE 61: *Check-Up*

VOCABULARY CHECK

1. government
2. branches
3. executive
4. legislative
5. judicial

DID YOU UNDERSTAND?

New Vocabulary: who

1. There are three branches of government in the United States.
2. The names of the branches of government are the legislative branch, the executive branch, and the judicial branch.
3. The President and Vice President work in the executive branch.
4. The Supreme Court justices work in the judicial branch.
5. Senators and representatives work in the legislative branch.

DISCUSSION

Have students describe the structure of the government in their native countries.

Making, Enforcing, and Explaining the Laws of the United States

FOCUS

> **TOPIC**
>
> Branches of Government
>
> **GRAMMAR**
>
> **Simple Present Tense**
>
> They **work** in the Capitol.
> The President **works** in the White House.

NEW VOCABULARY

Capitol	law
Congress	make
enforce	they
explain	White House

GETTING READY

Introduce the third person singular, present tense.

a. Write on the board:

> I work at *(name of school)*.
> The President works in the White House.

b. Model the sentences for students.

c. Have students repeat chorally and individually.

PREVIEWING THE STORY

Have students talk about the story title and the photographs to establish the context of the story. Ask some or all of the following questions:

> What do the three branches of the United States government do?
>
> (Point to the top picture.)
> What building is this?
> Where is it?
> What branch of government works there?
> Who works there?
>
> (Point to the middle picture.)
> What building is this?

> Where is it?
> What branch of government works there?
> Who works there?
>
> (Point to the bottom picture.)
> What building is this?
> Where is it?
> What branch of government works there?
> Who works there?

READING THE STORY

1. Have students read the story silently.

2. **Check Reading Comprehension:** Ask students a question about each line of the story. For beginning-level students, ask these questions in the order below so that the questions follow the sequence of the story. For higher-level students, ask the questions in random order.

   > What is the legislative branch of the government called?
   > Who's in the Congress?
   > What do they do?
   > Where does the Congress work?
   > Where is the Capitol?
   >
   > Who works in the executive branch?
   > What do the President and Vice President do?
   > Where does the President live and work?
   > Where is the White House?
   >
   > Who works in the judicial branch?
   > What do the Supreme Court justices do?
   > Where do the Supreme Court justices work?
   > Where is the Supreme Court?

3. Ask students if they have any questions about the story; check understanding of vocabulary.

4. **Choral Repetition:** Read aloud each line of the story and have students repeat.

5. **Class Circle Reading:** Have students read the story aloud as a class, with different students reading each line. (You can assign each line to a particular student or by seating patterns, or by letting students take turns spontaneously. In large classes, have a different group or row of students read each line.)

6. **Pair Practice:** Have students work in pairs, reading the passage to each other paragraph by paragraph. Circulate around the room and check students' reading and pronunciation, focusing more attention on students who need more assistance.

MATCHING I

1. the legislative branch
2. the executive branch
3. the judicial branch

MATCHING II

1. enforces the laws
2. explains the laws
3. makes the laws

MATCHING III

1. the judicial branch
2. the executive branch
3. the legislative branch

ANSWER THESE QUESTIONS

Students may answer these questions in different ways.

1. the legislative branch / the Congress / senators and representatives
2. the judicial branch / the Supreme Court / the Supreme Court justices
3. the executive branch / the President and Vice President

DISCUSSION

Have students discuss how the government works in their native countries. Then have them discuss U.S. laws they know about.

TEXT PAGES 64–65: INTERVIEW:

How Many Branches Does the United States Government Have?

FOCUS

TOPIC

Branches of Government

GRAMMAR

Can

Can you name the three branches?
Yes, I **can.**

Simple Present Tense

Which branch make**s** the laws?
Who work**s** in the legislative branch?

FUNCTIONAL INTERVIEW SKILLS

Reporting Information
Checking Understanding
Hesitating

NEW VOCABULARY

can	very good
tell	which
think	

GETTING READY

Introduce *can.*

Write on the board:

Can you _____?	Yes, I can.

a. Model the answer and have students repeat both chorally and individually.

b. Have several students answer, "Yes, I can" as you ask about their ability to speak their native language.

PRACTICING THE MODEL DIALOG

1. **Setting the Scene:** Have students look at the photograph and determine the subject of the conversation: "The INS examiner is asking questions about the branches of the United States government."

2. **Listening:** With books closed, have students listen to the dialog—presented by you, by a pair of students, or on the audio program.

3. **Choral Repetition:** With books still closed, model each line and have the whole class repeat in unison.

4. **Reading:** With books open, have students follow along as two students present the model dialog. Ask students if they have any questions and check understanding of vocabulary.

5. **Choral Conversation Practice:** Divide the class in half. Have Group 1 ask the questions and Group 2 give the answers; then reverse. (Or: You ask the questions and have the whole class answer in unison; then reverse.)

6. Call on one or two pairs of students to present the model dialog.

PRACTICING NEW DIALOGS

1. Call on one or two pairs of students to present new dialogs, using the information in the exercises and the skeletal dialog as a guide.

2. **Pair Practice:** Have students practice making new dialogs in pairs, taking turns being the INS examiner and the applicant.

3. Call on one or two more pairs of students to present their new dialogs to the class.

1. A. How many branches does the United States government have?
   B. The government has three branches.
   A. Can you name the three branches?
   B. Yes, I can. The legislative branch, the executive branch, and the judicial branch.
   A. And which branch *enforces* the laws of the United States?
   B. Which branch *enforces* the laws?
   A. Yes.
   B. Hmm. I think the *executive* branch *enforces* the laws.
   A. That's right. And can you tell me who works in the *executive* branch?
   B. *The President and the Vice President.*
   A. That's correct. Very good.

2. A. How many branches does the United States government have?
   B. The government has three branches.
   A. Can you name the three branches?
   B. Yes, I can. The legislative branch, the executive branch, and the judicial branch.
   A. And which branch *explains* the laws of the United States?
   B. Which branch *explains* the laws?
   A. Yes.
   B. Hmm. I think the *judicial* branch *explains* the laws.
   A. That's right. And can you tell me who works in the *judicial* branch?
   B. *The Supreme Court justices.*
   A. That's correct. Very good.

TEXT PAGE 66: *Check-Up*

GRAMMAR CHECK

1. lives
2. work
3. works
4. explain
5. enforces

QUESTIONS AND ANSWERS

This exercise offers students important practice with the multiple ways a question might be posed by the INS examiner. First, have students repeat each question after you. Then, have students practice asking and answering the questions with other students. Finally, have students write their answers to questions 1, 2, and 3.

1. The legislative branch.
2. The judicial branch.
3. The executive branch.

LISTENING

Have students complete the exercises as you play the audio program or read the following:

Listen and circle the correct answer.

1. Where does the president work?
2. Where does the Congress work?
3. Who makes the laws of the United States?
4. Who explains the laws of the United States?
5. Who enforces the laws of the United States?
6. Who works in the Congress of the United States?

Answers

1. White House
2. Capitol
3. Congress
4. Supreme Court
5. the President
6. senators

TEXT PAGE 67: *Review*

Have students work in pairs, taking turns asking and answering the questions. (For additional practice, students can write the answers to these questions on a separate sheet of paper.)

1. (Name of your state.)
2. (Name of your city or town.)
3. (Name of your state capital.)
4. Washington, D.C.
5. Yes, I do.
6. Fifty.

7. Thirteen.
8. Red, white, and blue.
9. The legislative branch / the Congress / senators and representatives.
10. In the White House.
11. Three.
12. The legislative branch, the executive branch, and the judicial branch.
13. It explains the laws.
14. The executive branch.
15. The judicial branch.

TEXT PAGES 68–69: *Chapter Test*

You can use this test as a standardized form of assessment to measure student achievement of the curriculum objectives in Chapter 3. The test consists of 20 multiple-choice items and five sentences for dictation.

To score the test on a scale of 100:

- For each correct multiple-choice item, score four points.

- For each dictation sentence, do a general evaluation of the correctness of words, spelling, punctuation, and legibility. Score each sentence as follows:

  4 (Excellent), **3** (Good), **2** (Fair), **1** (Poor), **0** (Unsatisfactory)

Students can write their answers in the text or on the reproducible Chapter Test Answer Sheet provided in the Appendix.

A. BRANCHES OF GOVERNMENT

1. A
2. C
3. B
4. A
5. D
6. D
7. C
8. A
9. D
10. C
11. B
12. B

B. GRAMMAR & VOCABULARY

13. C
14. A
15. C
16. B
17. D
18. A
19. B
20. C

C. DICTATION

Have students write these sentences as you read each sentence twice or play the audio program:

1. The president of the United States lives in the White House.
2. The White House is in Washington, D.C.
3. The Congress of the United States makes the laws.
4. The U.S. government has three branches.
5. Washington, D.C., is the capital of our country.

TEXT PAGE 70: *Civics Enrichment*

PERFORMANCE-BASED ASSESSMENT

These civics enrichment activities are designed to promote students' active participation in class and in the civic life of the community—through projects, issues discussions, community tasks, field trips, and Internet activities. Reproducible performance-based assessment forms for use in evaluating and documenting student participation in these activities are included in the Appendix.

CIVIC PARTICIPATION

Field Trip Preparation: Prepare students for a visit the class will make to the local office of your representative in the U.S. Congress. (The best timing for the visit is while students are working in the next chapter of the text.) Have students practice conversations in which they introduce themselves, tell where they are from, tell about when and why they came to the United States, describe what they are learning in school, and tell about their plans for the future.

COMMUNITY ISSUES

Have students brainstorm as a class problems or issues that are important to them. Have them discuss what they want to talk about and what opinions they want to share when they visit their representative.

INTERNET ACTIVITY

Have students go to the website listed in the text. This web page provides a list of all members of the U.S. House of Representatives with links to their websites. Have students find the link for their representative, go to the representative's website, and write down the kinds of information they find. Students can do this Internet activity individually, in pairs, or in small groups based on the computer resources available. Make sure students have the basic skills needed to access the Internet, such as using a computer keyboard and mouse and performing such tasks as clicking, scrolling, dragging, and typing URLs to access websites.

TECHNOLOGY ENRICHMENT

See Appendix page 159 for additional Internet enrichment activities related to this chapter.

CHAPTER 4

OVERVIEW
Student Text
Pages 71–84

TOPICS

The Congress
The President
The Supreme Court

GRAMMAR

Simple Present Tense vs. To Be
There Are
Time Expressions
Question Formation

FUNCTIONAL INTERVIEW SKILL

Reporting Information

KEY VOCABULARY

PEOPLE

armed forces
chief executive
Chief Justice of the
   United States
Commander-in-Chief
congressman
congressperson
congresswoman
judge
people
President
representative
senator
Supreme Court
   justices
Vice President

BRANCHES OF GOVERNMENT

Congress
executive branch
House of
   Representatives
judicial branch
legislative branch
Senate
Supreme Court
White House

QUESTION WORDS

how
how long
how many
what
when
where
which
who

OTHER WORDS

appoint
approve
at the same time
become
court
die
different
elect
enforce the laws
explain the laws
federal courts
fewer
government
head
highest
if
life
live
make the laws

many
more
name
new
part
serve
state
term
United States
work
year

FUNCTIONAL EXPRESSIONS

All right.
Can you name . . . ?
Do you know the
   name . . .?
Name . . .

RELATED PRACTICE

Foundations: Chapter 5
Word by Word Basic: pages 52–53, 146–149
Word by Word: pages 32, 84
Side by Side Book 1: Chapter 12
Side by Side Interactive CD-ROM / Side by Side TV Video: Level 1B, Segments 18, 19
ExpressWays Book 1: Chapter 5

TEXT PAGE 71: *Vocabulary Preview*

You may want to introduce these words before beginning the chapter, or you may choose to wait until they first occur in a specific lesson. If you choose to introduce them at this point, here are some suggestions:

1. Have students look at the photographs on text page 71 and identify the words they already know.

2. Present the vocabulary. Say each word and have the class repeat it chorally and individually. Check students' understanding and pronunciation of the words.

3. Practice the vocabulary as a class, in pairs, or in small groups. Have students cover the word list and look at the photographs. Practice the words in the following ways:

   • Say a word and have students tell the correct number on the photograph.
   • Give a number on a photograph and have students say the word.

TEXT PAGE 72: *The Congress of the United States*

FOCUS

> ### TOPIC
> The Congress
>
> ### GRAMMAR
> **There Are**
>
> **There are** one hundred senators.
>
> **Simple Present Tense vs. To Be**
>
> Representatives **work** in the House of Representatives.
> A representative **is** also called a congressperson.
>
> **Time Expressions**
>
> A senator's term is **six years.**
> A representative's term is **two years.**

NEW VOCABULARY

also	more
congressman	Senate
congressperson	six
congresswoman	term
different	year
fewer	
House of Representatives	

PREVIEWING THE STORY

Have students talk about the story title and the photograph to establish the context of the story. Ask some or all of the following questions:

What building is this?
Where is it?
Who works there?
Who are the senators from our state?
What's the name of our congressman/
  congresswoman/representative?
Who makes the laws in your native country?

READING THE STORY

1. Have students read the story silently.

2. **Check Reading Comprehension:** Ask students a question about each line of the story. For beginning-level students, ask these questions in the order below so that the questions follow the sequence of the story. For higher-level students, ask the questions in random order.

   What is the Congress of the United States?
   Who makes the laws of the United States?
   What are the two parts of the Congress?

   Who works in the Senate?
   How many senators are there?
   How many senators are there from each state?
   How long is a senator's term?

   Where do representatives work?
   What are representatives also called?
   How many representatives are there?
   Does each state have the same number of representatives?
   Which states have more representatives?
   Which states have fewer representatives?
   How long is a representative's term?

3. Ask students if they have any questions about the story; check understanding of vocabulary.

4. **Choral Repetition:** Read aloud each line of the story and have students repeat.

5. **Class Circle Reading:** Have students read the story aloud as a class, with different students reading each line. (You can assign each line to a particular student or by seating patterns, or by letting students take turns spontaneously. In large classes, have a different group or row of students read each line.)

6. **Pair Practice:** Have students work in pairs, reading the passage to each other paragraph by paragraph. Circulate around the room and check students' reading and pronunciation, focusing more attention on students who need more assistance.

EXPANSION

1. Bring in an electoral map of the United States and discuss the number of representatives from various states, including your own. Have students find out the names of your states' senators and the representative from your district.

2. Bring in or have students bring in pictures of senators and representatives from newspapers and magazines.

TEXT PAGE 73: *Check-Up*

VOCABULARY CHECK

1. legislative
2. senators
3. representatives
4. six
5. two
6. congresswomen

DID YOU UNDERSTAND?

New Vocabulary: how long

1. The legislative branch. / The Congress.
2. The Senate and the House of Representatives.
3. One hundred (100).
4. 435.
5. (Answer for your state.)
6. Two years.
7. Two (2). (Not applicable to Washington, D.C.)
8. Six years.

Who Makes the Laws of the United States?

FOCUS

TOPIC

The Congress

GRAMMAR

Simple Present Tense vs. To Be

Who **makes** the laws of the United States?
What **are** the two parts of the Congress called?

FUNCTIONAL INTERVIEW SKILL

Reporting Information

NEW VOCABULARY

about
ask

GETTING READY

Review the names of your senators and
representative.

PRACTICING THE DIALOG

1. **Setting the Scene:** Have students look at the
   photograph and determine the subject of the
   conversation: "The INS examiner is asking
   questions about the Congress."

2. **Filling In Information:** Have students fill in
   the names of their senators and representatives
   on the appropriate lines.

3. **Listening:** With books closed, have students
   listen to the dialog—presented by you, by a pair
   of students, or on the audio program.

4. **Choral Repetition:** With books still closed,
   model each line and have the whole class repeat
   in unison.

5. **Reading:** With books open, have students follow
   along as two students present the model dialog.
   Ask students if they have any questions and
   check understanding of vocabulary.

6. **Choral Conversation Practice:** Divide the
   class in half. Have Group 1 ask the questions
   and Group 2 give the answers; then reverse. (Or:
   You ask the questions and have the whole class
   answer in unison; then reverse.)

7. Call on one or two pairs of students to present
   the dialog.

8. **Pair Practice:** Have students practice the
   dialog in pairs, taking turns being the INS
   examiner and the applicant.

9. Call on one or two more pairs of students to
   present the dialog to the class.

FOCUS

> ### TOPIC
> The President
>
> ### GRAMMAR
>
> **Simple Present Tense vs. To Be**
>
> The President **is** the chief executive.
> The President **lives** and **works** in the
>   White House.
>
> **Time Expressions**
>
> The President's term is **four years.**
> The American people elect a president
>   **every four years.**

NEW VOCABULARY

> | | |
> |---|---|
> | armed forces | head |
> | become | if |
> | chief executive | people |
> | Commander-in-Chief | serve |
> | die | the same time |
> | elect | with |

GETTING READY

Write on the board:

1996	1998	2000	2002	2004
1997	1999	2001	2003	2005

Say, "We elected a president in 1996 and in 2000.
We elect one in 2004 and 2008. We elect a president
every four years."

PREVIEWING THE STORY

Have students talk about the story title and the
photograph to establish the context of the story. Ask
some or all of the following questions:

Who is this man?
What's his name?/What's his job?
Does your native country have a president?

READING THE STORY

1. Have students read the story silently.

2. **Check Reading Comprehension:** Ask
    students a question about each line of the story.
    For beginning-level students, ask these questions
    in the order below so that the questions follow
    the sequence of the story. For higher-level
    students, ask the questions in random order.

    Who is the head of the executive branch of the
        government?
    What does the executive branch do?
    Who is the chief executive?
    Who is Commander-in-Chief of the armed
        forces?

    Where does the President live and work?
    How long is the President's term?
    When/How often do the American people elect
        a president?
    How many terms can the President serve?

    What does the Vice President do?
    When do the American people elect the Vice
        President?
    If the President dies, who becomes the new
        President?

    What is the name of the President?
    What is the name of the Vice President?

3. Ask students if they have any questions about
    the story; check understanding of vocabulary.

4. **Choral Repetition:** Read aloud each line of the
    story and have students repeat.

5. **Class Circle Reading:** Have students read the
    story aloud as a class, with different students
    reading each line. (You can assign each line to a
    particular student or by seating patterns, or by
    letting students take turns spontaneously. In
    large classes, have a different group or row of
    students read each line.)

6. **Pair Practice:** Have students work in pairs,
    reading the passage to each other paragraph by
    paragraph. Circulate around the room and check
    students' reading and pronunciation, focusing
    more attention on students who need more
    assistance.

EXPANSION

1. Vocabulary Expansion

Have students look again at the photograph on page 75. Ask them if they know what day is shown in the photograph (Inauguration Day). Have them describe what is happening in the photograph. (The President is taking the "oath of office.") Have them point to the Chief Justice, the First Lady, and the President's children.

2. Language Experience Letter

Have students dictate a letter to the President expressing their opinion on a national or world issue. As you ask students for the following information, write what they say on the board or on a large sheet of paper. (Since the focus is on self-expression, do not dwell on grammatical corrections at this point. Either take down the students' responses verbatim or incorporate corrections without drawing attention to them.) You can write one letter for the entire class, various letters for small groups, or letters for individual students.

a. Have students discuss what national or world issue they wish to write about to the President.

b. Ask students the following questions, writing down the answers in a letter format:

What's today's date?
Who are you writing to? (Write "Dear President _____")
What is your opinion?
Why do you think that?

Finish the letter by adding "Thank you for your attention" and "Sincerely, (Name)."

c. Read the letter to the class (or small group). Point to each word or sentence as you read. Then have students repeat each sentence after you.

d. Write down the letters on regular-sized paper. Make copies for each student in the class.

e. You may want to consider sending students' letters to the President. The address is:

The White House
1600 Pennsylvania Avenue, N.W.
Washington, D.C. 20500

TEXT PAGE 76: *Check-Up*

VOCABULARY CHECK

1. White House
2. elect
3. armed forces
4. serve
5. executive

THE ANSWER IS "THE PRESIDENT!"

1. The President.
2. The President.
3. The President.
4. The President.

WHAT'S THE NUMBER?

1. 6
2. 2
3. 2
4. 4
5. 100
6. 435

FOCUS

TOPIC

The Supreme Court

GRAMMAR

Simple Present Tense vs. To Be

The judicial branch **explains** the laws of the
    United States.
They **serve** for life.
The American people **don't elect** the
    Supreme Court justices.

The Supreme Court **is** the highest court in
    the United States.
They **are** also called Supreme Court justices.

There Are

There are nine judges in the Supreme Court.

Time Expressions

They serve **for life.**

NEW VOCABULARY

appoint	court	highest
approve	don't	life
Chief Justice	federal court	them

PREVIEWING THE STORY

Have students talk about the story title and the
photograph to establish the context of the story. Ask
some or all of the following questions:

How many people are there in this photograph?
Who are they?
What do they do?
Where is the Supreme Court?
Is there a supreme court in your native country?

READING THE STORY

1. Have students read the story silently.

2. **Check Reading Comprehension:** Ask
students a question about each line of the story.
For beginning-level students, ask these questions
in the order below so that the questions follow
the sequence of the story. For higher-level
students, ask the questions in random order.

What is the judicial branch of the government?
What does the judicial branch do?
What is the highest court in the United
    States?
How many judges are there in the Supreme
    Court?
What is another name for the judges in the
    Supreme Court? / What are Supreme Court
    judges also called?
How long do they serve?
Do the American people elect the Supreme
    Court justices?
Who appoints them? Who approves them?

What is the head of the Supreme Court called?
What is the name of the Chief Justice of the
    United States?

3. Ask students if they have any questions about
the story; check understanding of vocabulary.

4. **Choral Repetition:** Read aloud each line of the
story and have students repeat.

5. **Class Circle Reading:** Have students read the
story aloud as a class, with different students
reading each line. (You can assign each line to a
particular student or by seating patterns, or by
letting students take turns spontaneously. In
large classes, have a different group or row of
students read each line.)

6. **Pair Practice:** Have students work in pairs,
reading the passage to each other paragraph by
paragraph. Circulate around the room and check
students' reading and pronunciation, focusing
more attention on students who need more
assistance.

EXPANSION

1. Have students discuss why the Supreme Court is
important.

2. Discuss with students an issue currently being
considered by the Supreme Court. Or discuss an
important Supreme Court ruling from recent
history.

3. **Internet Activity:** Have students use an
Internet search engine (such as
www.yahoo.com) to find the names of the
current Supreme Court justices.

DID YOU UNDERSTAND?

Have students answer these questions in full sentences.

> 1. The Supreme Court is the highest court in the United States.
> 2. It is in the judicial branch of the government.
> 3. There are nine judges in the Supreme Court.
> 4. The President appoints the Supreme Court justices.
> 5. The Chief Justice is the head of the Supreme Court.
> 6. The Chief Justice of the United States is _____.

GRAMMAR CHECK

Before doing this exercise review the meanings of the question words in the box. Have students make up questions using these words, and have other students answer the questions.

> 1. How many
> 2. How long
> 3. Who
> 4. What
> 5. Where

After filling in the answers, have students practice asking and answering the questions.

QUESTIONS AND ANSWERS

This exercise offers students important practice with the multiple ways a question might be posed by the INS examiner. First, have students repeat each question after you. Then, have students practice asking and answering the questions with other students. Finally, have students write their answers to questions 1–5.

LISTENING

In order to do the listening exercise, students will first need to write the name of the President on line A, the name of a senator on line B, and the name of the Chief Justice on line C.

Then have students complete the exercises as you play the audio program or read the following:

> *Listen and circle A, B, or C.*
>
> 1. Who's the Commander-in-Chief of the armed forces?
> 2. Who works in the Congress of the United States?
> 3. Who explains the laws of the United States?
> 4. Who works in the White House?
> 5. Who makes the laws of the United States?
> 6. Who don't the American people elect?
>
> **Answers**
>
> | | |
> |---|---|
> | 1. A | 4. A |
> | 2. B | 5. B |
> | 3. C | 6. C |

TEXT PAGE 80: *Civic Participation*

WRITE A LETTER

Have each student write a letter to the President, a representative, or a senator.

YOU'RE THE JUDGE!

Simulation: Have the class appoint nine Supreme Court justices to decide on an issue relating to immigrant rights or another matter of interest to your students. Give the "justices" time to deliberate and then have them report their decisions to the class.

MEET WITH YOUR REPRESENTATIVE IN CONGRESS

Invite your district's representative or a staff person to visit your school, or arrange a class visit to your representative's local office. Have students introduce themselves, give some personal background information, and talk about what they are learning in your class. Have them also prepare questions to ask the representative about his or her job.

Branches of Government

1. Help students read the chart by pointing out the vertical and horizontal headings and reviewing what they mean.

2. Point to a particular box of information on the chart and have students give a full sentence containing that information. For example:

Point to:	Full Sentence:
100	There are 100 senators.
6 years	A senator's term is six years.
Senate	Senators work in the Senate.
Make the laws	The legislative branch makes the laws of the United States.

3. Have students practice asking and answering the first set of questions based on the chart.

4. Have students practice asking and answering the second set of questions about the names of people in the government.

TEXT PAGES 82–83: *Chapter Test*

You can use this test as a standardized form of assessment to measure student achievement of the curriculum objectives in Chapter 4. The test consists of 20 multiple-choice items and five sentences for dictation.

To score the test on a scale of 100:

- For each correct multiple-choice item, score four points.

- For each dictation sentence, do a general evaluation of the correctness of words, spelling, punctuation, and legibility. Score each sentence as follows:

  4 (Excellent), **3** (Good), **2** (Fair), **1** (Poor), **0** (Unsatisfactory)

Students can write their answers in the text or on the reproducible Chapter Test Answer Sheet provided in the Appendix.

A. THE CONGRESS, THE PRESIDENT, & THE SUPREME COURT

1. B
2. D
3. A
4. C
5. A
6. D
7. B
8. B
9. D
10. A
11. B
12. C

B. GRAMMAR: QUESTION WORDS

13. B
14. D
15. B
16. C
17. A
18. D
19. A
20. C

C. DICTATION

Have students write these sentences as you read each sentence twice or play the audio program:

1. The president and the vice president work in the White House.
2. I'm studying about the president of the United States.
3. There are one hundred (100) senators.
4. The Supreme Court explains the laws.
5. We elect a president every four years.

TEXT PAGE 84: *Civics Enrichment*

PERFORMANCE-BASED ASSESSMENT

These civics enrichment activities are designed to promote students' active participation in class and in the civic life of the community—through projects, issues discussions, community tasks, field trips, and Internet activities. Reproducible performance-based assessment forms for use in evaluating and documenting student participation in these activities are included in the Appendix.

CIVIC PARTICIPATION

Field Trip or Classroom Visitor: Visit the local office of your students' representative in the U.S. Congress. During the visit, have students introduce themselves, tell where they are from, tell about when and why they came to the United States, describe what they are learning in school, and tell about their plans for the future. Have students also share some of the problems, issues, and opinions that they brainstormed in class (a civics enrichment activity in the previous chapter). As an alternative to the field trip, you might arrange for the representative to visit your classroom.

INTERNET ACTIVITY

Online Field Trip to the U.S. Capitol: Have students go to the website listed in the text for the U.S. House of Representatives. Have students click on "Visiting the Nation's Capital." Then have them click on "Virtual Tour of Capitol" and go on the tour. Students should make a list or write short sentences about what they see on the virtual tour. Students can do this Internet activity individually, in pairs, or in small groups based on the computer resources available. Make sure students have the basic skills needed to access the Internet, such as using a computer keyboard and mouse and performing such tasks as clicking, scrolling, dragging, and typing URLs to access websites.

INTERNET ACTIVITY

Visiting the White House Online: Have students go to the website listed in the text for the President of the United States. Have them click on "Your Government," read about the President's Cabinet and the branches of government, and write down some of the key information (such as the names of current Cabinet officials). Then have students go to the News and Features section of the website, click on "Photo Essays," look at the photographs and captions, and write sentences about what they see.

TECHNOLOGY ENRICHMENT

See Appendix page 159 for additional Internet enrichment activities related to this chapter.

<table>
<tr>
<td>

CHAPTER 5

</td>
<td>

OVERVIEW
Student Text
Pages 85–98

</td>
</tr>
</table>

TOPICS

Types of Government
State & Local Government
Public Officials
The Constitution
The Bill of Rights

GRAMMAR

Review:
  To Be
  Simple Present Tense
  Have/Has
  There Are
  Can
  WH-Questions
  Yes/No Questions

FUNCTIONAL INTERVIEW SKILL

Reporting Information

KEY VOCABULARY

GOVERNMENT

branch	local
city	monarchy
county	queen
democratic	representative
dictator	republic
dictatorship	state
federal	state courts
form of government	state legislature
government	town
king	United States
level of government	government

THE CONSTITUTION & BILL OF RIGHTS

amendment	freedoms
Bill of Rights	law
Constitution	meet together
First Amendment	rights
freedom of assembly	rule
freedom of religion	say
freedom of speech	worship
freedom of the press	write

PUBLIC OFFICIALS		OTHER WORDS		
Chief Justice of the United States	official President	build change	highest house	public schools sales taxes
city manager	public official	driver's license	immigration	serve
congressperson	representative	elect	included	Social Security
governor	Senate	enforce the laws	makes the laws	taxes
House of Representatives	senator Supreme Court	explain the laws garbage collection	parking regulations people	vote work
mayor	Vice President	guaranteed	permission	

RELATED PRACTICE

Foundations: Chapter 6
Word by Word Basic: pages 56–67
Word by Word: pages 34–39
Side by Side Book 1: Chapters 13, 14
Side by Side Interactive CD-ROM / Side by Side TV Video: Level 1B, Segments 20–23
ExpressWays Book 1: Chapter 5

TEXT PAGE 85: *Vocabulary Preview*

You may want to introduce these words before beginning the chapter, or you may choose to wait until they first occur in a specific lesson. If you choose to introduce them at this point, here are some suggestions:

1. Have students look at the photographs on text page 85 and identify the words they already know.

2. Present the vocabulary. Say each word and have the class repeat it chorally and individually. Check students' understanding and pronunciation of the words.

3. Practice the vocabulary as a class, in pairs, or in small groups. Have students cover the word list and look at the photographs. Practice the words in the following ways:

• Say a word and have students tell the number of the photograph.
• Give the number of a photograph and have students say the word.

TEXT PAGE 86: *A Representative Form of Government*

FOCUS

TOPIC

Types of Government

GRAMMAR

To Be

The United States **is** a republic.
The United States **is not** a dictatorship.

Simple Present Tense

The American people **vote** for public officials.

Have/Has

It **has** a democratic form of government.
It **doesn't have** a dictator.

NEW VOCABULARY

democratic	monarchy
dictator	official
dictatorship	queen
doesn't	republic
king	these

PREVIEWING THE STORY

Have students talk about the story title and the photograph to establish the context of the story. Ask some or all of the following questions:

   What's she doing?
   What's she using to vote?
   Where is the voting machine?
   Who do you think she is voting for?
   When does she vote?
   Do people vote in your native country?
   When?
   How?

READING THE STORY

1. Have students read the story silently.
2. **Check Reading Comprehension:** Ask students a question about each line of the story. For beginning-level students, ask these questions in the order below so that the questions follow the sequence of the story. For higher-level students, ask the questions in random order.

   Is the United States a dictatorship?
   Does it have a dictator?
   Is the United States a monarchy?
   Does it have a king or a queen?

   What is the United States?
   What form of government does the United States have?
   Does the United States have a representative form of government?

   Who votes for public officials?
   Who do the American people elect?
   Where do these officials work?
   Who do they serve?

3. Ask students if they have any questions about the story; check understanding of vocabulary.
4. **Choral Repetition:** Read aloud each line of the story and have students repeat.
5. **Class Circle Reading:** Have students read the story aloud as a class, with different students reading each line. (You can assign each line to a particular student or by seating patterns, or by letting students take turns spontaneously. In large classes, have a different group or row of students read each line.)
6. **Pair Practice:** Have students work in pairs, reading the passage to each other paragraph by paragraph. Circulate around the room and check students' reading and pronunciation, focusing more attention on students who need more assistance.

VOCABULARY CHECK

1. democratic
2. elect
3. serve
4. monarchy
5. republic

GRAMMAR CHECK

1. doesn't
2. isn't
3. has
4. elect
5. serves

DID YOU UNDERSTAND?

1. It has a democratic form of government./
   It has a representative form of government.
2. It is a republic.
3. The American people elect them.
4. They elect the President, the Vice President,
   the senators, and the congressmen and
   congresswomen.

HOW ABOUT YOU?

Have students discuss the types of government and
elections in their countries.

TEXT PAGE 88: *State and Local Government*

FOCUS

TOPICS

State and Local Government
Public Officials

GRAMMAR

Have/Has

The federal government **has** three branches.
Most state governments also **have** three
   branches.

There Are

There are many kinds of local government.
There are cities, towns, and counties.

Simple Present Tense

The state legislature **makes** the laws.
The state courts **explain** the laws of the state.

To Be

The governor **is** the head of the state's
   government.

NEW VOCABULARY

city manager	level
county	local
governor	mayor
kind	state legislature

GETTING READY

The Three Levels of Government

Draw on the board representations of the U.S.
Capitol, your state's capitol building, and your city
or town hall. Eliciting as much of the information
as possible from the class, fill in the following
information under each building:

   what the building is called;
   where the building is located;
   who heads the government;
   what that level of government is called.

At the conclusion of this activity, the board should
look as follows:

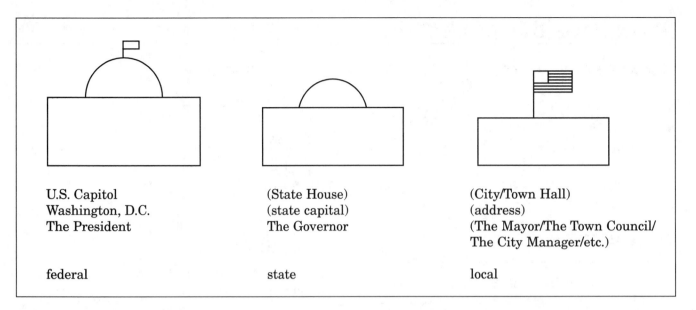

U.S. Capitol
Washington, D.C.
The President

(State House)
(state capital)
The Governor

(City/Town Hall)
(address)
(The Mayor/The Town Council/
The City Manager/etc.)

federal

state

local

PREVIEWING THE STORY

Have students talk about the story title and the
photographs to establish the context of the story.
Ask some or all of the following questions:

(Point to the photograph on the left.)
Is this the United States Capitol in Washington,
D.C.?
(If students answer "Yes," show them the
picture of the U.S. Capitol on page 72.)
Where do you think this is? (Austin, Texas)

(Point to the photograph on the right.)
Is this the United States Capitol in Washington,
D.C.?
(If students answer "Yes," show them the
picture of the U.S. Capitol on page 72.)
Where do you think this is? (Sacramento,
California)

Where's the capital of the United States?
What's the name of our state?
Where's the capital of our state?

READING THE STORY

1. Have students read the story silently.

2. **Check Reading Comprehension:** Ask
students a question about each line of the story.
For beginning-level students, ask these questions
in the order below so that the questions follow
the sequence of the story. For higher-level
students, ask the questions in random order.

What are the three levels of government in the
United States?

How many branches does the federal
government have?

How many branches do most state
governments have?

What does the state legislature do?
What do the state courts do?
Who is the head of the state's government?
What does the governor do?
What is the name of our state?
What is the name of our governor?

Are all the local governments in the United
States the same?
What kinds of local governments are there?
Who is the head of the local government in
some cities and towns?
Who is the head of the local government in
other cities and towns?
What is the name of our city/town?
What is the name of our mayor/city manager?
What is the name of our county?

3. Ask students if they have any questions about
the story; check understanding of vocabulary.

4. **Choral Repetition:** Read aloud each line of the
story and have students repeat.

5. **Class Circle Reading:** Have students read the
story aloud as a class, with different students
reading each line. (You can assign each line to a
particular student or by seating patterns, or by
letting students take turns spontaneously. In
large classes, have a different group or row of
students read each line.)

6. **Pair Practice:** Have students work in pairs,
reading the passage to each other paragraph by
paragraph. Circulate around the room and check
students' reading and pronunciation, focusing
more attention on students who need more
assistance.

VOCABULARY CHECK

1. local
2. governor
3. mayor
4. state legislature
5. state courts

DID YOU UNDERSTAND?

Have students provide short answers to these questions.

1. The governor.
2. The state legislature.
3. (Answer depends on locality.)
4. Federal, state, and local.
5. Legislative, executive, and judicial.

FEDERAL, STATE, OR LOCAL?

a. State	e. Federal
b. Local	f. Local
c. Federal	g. State and Local
d. Local	h. Local

CIVIC PARTICIPATION

As a class, have students write a letter to a local government official. Have them explain that they are studying English and Civics, and have them request a meeting with the official and a tour of the local government offices. (This letter sets up the Civic Participation Field Trip on text page 98.)

TEXT PAGES 90–91: INTERVIEW:
What City or Town Do You Live in?

FOCUS

TOPICS

State and Local Government
Public Officials

GRAMMAR

WH-Questions

What city or town do you live in?
Who makes the laws in Orange County?

Can

Can you name the governor of your state?

Yes/No Questions

Do you know the mayor's name?

FUNCTIONAL INTERVIEW SKILL

Reporting Information

NEW VOCABULARY

Board of Supervisors
city council
leader

GETTING READY

Review the names of your state's governor and the head of your local government.

PRACTICING THE MODEL DIALOG

1. **Setting the Scene:** Have students look at the photograph and determine the subject of the conversation: "The INS examiner is asking questions about state and local government."
2. **Listening:** With books closed, have students listen to the dialog—presented by you, by a pair of students, or on the audio program.
3. **Choral Repetition:** With books still closed, model each line and have the whole class repeat in unison.

4. **Reading:** With books open, have students follow along as two students present the model dialog. Ask students if they have any questions and check understanding of vocabulary.

5. **Choral Conversation Practice:** Divide the class in half. Have Group 1 ask the questions and Group 2 give the answers; then reverse. (Or: You ask the questions and have the whole class answer in unison; then reverse.)

6. Call on one or two pairs of students to present the model dialog.

PRACTICING NEW DIALOGS

1. Call on one or two pairs of students to present new dialogs, using the skeletal dialog as a guide and filling in the blanks with the appropriate information.

2. **Pair Practice:** Have students practice making new dialogs in pairs, taking turns being the INS examiner and the applicant.

3. Call on one or two more pairs of students to present their new dialogs to the class.

TEXT PAGE 92: *The Constitution*

FOCUS

> ### TOPIC
> The Constitution
>
> ### GRAMMAR
>
> **Simple Present Tense vs. To Be**
>
> The Constitution **gives** the rules for the three branches of government.
> The Constitution **is** the highest law in the United States.

NEW VOCABULARY

Constitution	own
do	rule
give	tell
help	

PREVIEWING THE STORY

Have students talk about the story title and the photograph to establish the context of the story. Ask some or all of the following questions:

Say, "This is a very important document in the United States."
What is the name of this document?
Why is it important?
How old is it?
Does your native country have a constitution?
How old is it?

READING THE STORY

1. Have students read the story silently.

2. **Check Reading Comprehension:** Ask students a question about each line of the story. For beginning-level students, ask these questions in the order below so that the questions follow the sequence of the story. For higher-level students, ask the questions in random order.

    What is the Constitution?
    What is the Constitution called?

    What gives the rules for the three branches of government?
    What does the Constitution say?
    What does the Constitution tell the Senate and the House of Representatives?
    What does the Constitution tell the President and the Vice President?
    What does it help the Supreme Court do?
    Can states make their own laws?

3. Ask students if they have any questions about the story; check understanding of vocabulary.

4. **Choral Repetition:** Read aloud each line of the story and have students repeat.

5. **Class Circle Reading:** Have students read the story aloud as a class, with different students reading each line. (You can assign each line to a particular student or by seating patterns, or by letting students take turns spontaneously. In large classes, have a different group or row of students read each line.)

6. **Pair Practice:** Have students work in pairs, reading the passage to each other paragraph by paragraph. Circulate around the room and check students' reading and pronunciation, focusing more attention on students who need more assistance.

EXPANSION

1. Bring in a copy of the Constitution. Show students the various articles of the Constitution and describe what the articles are about. Pocket-sized copies of the Constitution can be obtained at many federal offices.

2. Have a "Constitutional Convention" in class. Have students write a constitution for their class or their school. Have them decide who should have which powers and responsibilities.

3. Have students describe their native country's constitution.

TEXT PAGE 93: *The Bill of Rights*

FOCUS

> **TOPIC**
>
> The Bill of Rights
>
> **GRAMMAR**
>
> **There Are**
>
> **There are** 27 amendments to the Constitution.
>
> **Can**
>
> Americans **can** say what they want to.

NEW VOCABULARY

all	guarantee	speech
amendment	important	together
assembly	meet	write
Bill of Rights	press	worship
change	religion	
freedom	right	

PREVIEWING THE STORY

Have students talk about the story title and the photograph to establish the context of the story. Ask some or all of the following questions:

> What freedoms and rights do you have because you live in the United States?
> Does the United States government control the newspapers?
> Can you go to any place of worship you want to?
> What can you do if you do not agree with the President?
> Do people have the same freedoms and rights in your native country?

READING THE STORY

1. Have students read the story silently.

2. **Check Reading Comprehension:** Ask students a question about each line of the story. For beginning-level students, ask these questions in the order below so that the questions follow the sequence of the story. For higher-level students, ask the questions in random order.

> Can the people of the United States change the Constitution?
> What are changes in the Constitution called?
> How many amendments to the Constitution are there?
> What are the first ten amendments called?
> What does the Bill of Rights give to all people in the United States?
> Which amendment gives Americans many important rights?
> Which amendment guarantees freedom of speech?
> What is freedom of speech?
> Which amendment guarantees freedom of the press?
> What is freedom of the press?
> Which amendment guarantees freedom of religion?
> What is freedom of religion?
> Which amendment guarantees freedom of assembly?
> What is freedom of assembly?

3. Ask students if they have any questions about the story; check understanding of vocabulary.

4. **Choral Repetition:** Read aloud each line of the story and have students repeat.

5. **Class Circle Reading:** Have students read the story aloud as a class, with different students reading each line. (You can assign each line to a particular student or by seating patterns, or by letting students take turns spontaneously. In large classes, have a different group or row of students read each line.)

6. **Pair Practice:** Have students work in pairs, reading the passage to each other paragraph by paragraph. Circulate around the room and check students' reading and pronunciation, focusing more attention on students who need more assistance.

TEXT PAGE 94: *Check-Up*

"MIRROR" QUESTIONS

Point out to students that the questions in the box are two different ways of asking about the same information. Have students practice both questions and answers, chorally and individually.

After students have written the answers to the questions on a separate sheet of paper, have them work in pairs, asking and answering the questions. Students can provide short answers to these questions.

1. Amendments.
2. Changes in the Constitution.
3. The Bill of Rights.
4. The first ten amendments to the Constitution.
5. The Constitution.
6. The supreme law of the land.

ANSWER THESE QUESTIONS

1. Yes
2. 27.
3. The first.

BILL OF RIGHTS PRACTICE

Students should choose from the following rights:

Freedom of speech
Freedom of the press
Freedom of religion
Freedom of assembly

DISCUSSION AND DEBATE

Lead a student discussion about equal rights and freedoms in the United States. Then lead a second discussion about limits on freedom of speech or other rights. You may want to conduct class debates on one or both issues.

TEXT PAGE 95: *Review*

LISTEN CAREFULLY!

Have students complete the exercises as you play the audio program or read the following:

These questions sound the same, but they are very different. Listen carefully and circle the correct answer.

1. What's the highest court in the United States?
2. What's the highest law in the United States?
3. What are the three levels of government in the United States?
4. What are the three branches of the United States government?
5. Which branch of government enforces the laws?
6. Which branch of government explains the laws?

Answers

1. the Supreme Court
2. the Constitution
3. federal, state, and local
4. legislative, executive, and judicial
5. the executive branch
6. the judicial branch

ADDITIONAL PRACTICE

Have students work in pairs, taking turns asking and answering the questions. (For additional practice, students can write the answers to these questions on a separate sheet of paper.)

1. (Name of your city or town)
2. (Name of your county)
3. (Name of your state)
4. (Name of your governor)
5. The state legislature.
6. The legislative branch / the Congress / senators and representatives.
7. 100.
8. (Names of the two U.S. senators from your state)
9. 435.
10. (Number of representatives from your state in the U.S. House of Representatives)
11. (Name of your congressperson in the House of Representatives)
12. (Name of the Chief Justice of the United States)
13. (Name of the President)
14. (Name of the Vice President)

You can use this test as a standardized form of assessment to measure student achievement of the curriculum objectives in Chapter 5. The test consists of 20 multiple-choice items and five sentences for dictation.

To score the test on a scale of 100:

- For each correct multiple-choice item, score four points.

- For each dictation sentence, do a general evaluation of the correctness of words, spelling, punctuation, and legibility. Score each sentence as follows:

  4 (Excellent), **3** (Good), **2** (Fair), **1** (Poor), **0** (Unsatisfactory)

Students can write their answers in the text or on the reproducible Chapter Test Answer Sheet provided in the Appendix.

A. GOVERNMENT, THE CONSTITUTION, & THE BILL OF RIGHTS

1. A
2. B
3. C
4. D
5. B
6. D
7. D
8. B
9. A
10. D
11. C
12. B

B. GRAMMAR & VOCABULARY

13. B
14. C
15. A
16. D
17. C
18. B
19. C
20. A

C. DICTATION

Have students write these sentences as you read each sentence twice or play the audio program:

1. I am studying the Constitution of the United States.

2. There are twenty-seven (27) amendments to the Constitution.

3. The first ten (10) amendments are the Bill of Rights.

4. The Constitution gives rights to all people in the United States.

5. The first amendment gives Americans freedom of speech.

PERFORMANCE-BASED ASSESSMENT

These civics enrichment activities are designed to promote students' active participation in class and in the civic life of the community—through projects, issues discussions, community tasks, field trips, and Internet activities. Reproducible performance-based assessment forms for use in evaluating and documenting student participation in these activities are included in the Appendix.

CIVIC PARTICIPATION

Field Trip: Arrange for your class to visit your city hall or town government office and to meet with a local official. The visit should include a tour of the building and an explanation of the services available in different departments of the local government. As preparation for the field trip, or as an alternative, students can visit the local government's website and learn about the different services available.

PROJECT ACTIVITY

"Class Election Day" Simulation: In this simulation, students conduct an election in class for the offices of class president and class vice president. Students nominate other students (or themselves) to be candidates. All students should participate in some aspect of the election process: candidates should give campaign speeches, students who serve on the Board of Elections should supervise the voting and count the ballots, some students should be TV news reporters who interview the candidates and report the election results, and other students should be voters. Have students take responsibility for all aspects of the Election Day simulation. Have them identify and assign the roles to be played and determine how to proceed with each stage of the election process. Be available to answer students' questions or to give advice when needed. Use the simulation as a basis for building students' skills in leadership, teamwork, and communicating information—key SCANS* skills useful for success in the workplace.

*Secretary's Commission on Achieving Necessary Skills

COMMUNITY ISSUES

Discussion: Have students discuss why it is important to vote in elections. Have them also explore rights and responsibilities, such as the right to vote and the responsibility of voters to be informed. If you wish to expand this discussion, you can have students talk about differences between elections in the United States and in their countries.

TECHNOLOGY ENRICHMENT

See Appendix page 159 for additional Internet enrichment activities related to this chapter.

<table>
<tr><td>

CHAPTER 6

</td><td>

OVERVIEW
Student Text
Pages 99–116

</td></tr>
</table>

TOPICS

Discovery
Colonization

GRAMMAR

Past Tense: Regular Verbs
Past Tense: Irregular Verbs
Did/Didn't

FUNCTIONAL INTERVIEW SKILLS

Reporting Information
Giving Partial Answers to Difficult Questions
Hesitating

KEY VOCABULARY

PEOPLE	PLACES	VERBS	
children	America	arrive	help
Christopher Columbus	Atlantic Coast	bring	hope
colonist	Atlantic Ocean	build	invite
European	colony	call	kill
family	England	celebrate	land (v.)
Indian	Europe	come	learn
Native American	homesite	come together	like
native people	the Indies	die	order
people	island	discover	punish
Pilgrim	Jamestown colony	eat	sail
settler	Jamestown, Virginia	find	sell
slave	North America	fish (v.)	ship (v.)
	Plimoth Plantation	get there	teach
FOOD	Plymouth colony	give thanks	trade
corn	Plymouth, Massachusetts	go	travel
cranberries	Spain	grow	want
potatoes	state	have	
squash	village		
turkey			

because
celebration
colonial
dinner
fort
gold

holiday
holiday tradition
life
Mayflower
parade

religious freedom
ship
Thanksgiving
Thanksgiving Day
tobacco

RELATED PRACTICE

Foundations: Chapter 8
Word by Word Basic: pages 76–81
Word by Word: pages 44–49
Side by Side Book 1: Chapter 15
Side by Side Interactive CD-ROM / Side by Side TV Video: Level 1B, Segment 24
ExpressWays Book 1: Chapter 6

TEXT PAGE 99: *Vocabulary Preview*

You may want to introduce these words before beginning the chapter, or you may choose to wait until they first occur in a specific lesson. If you choose to introduce them at this point, here are some suggestions:

1. Have students look at the photographs on text page 99 and identify the words they already know.

2. Present the vocabulary. Say each word and have the class repeat it chorally and individually. Check students' understanding and pronunciation of the words.

3. Practice the vocabulary as a class, in pairs, or in small groups. Have students cover the word list and look at the photographs. Practice the words in the following ways:

   • Say a word or name and have students tell the correct number on the photograph.
   • Give a number on a photograph and have students say the word or name.

FOCUS

TOPIC

Discovery

GRAMMAR

Past Tense: Regular Verbs

Christopher Columbus sail**ed** from Spain.
He want**ed** to go to the Indies.
People in Europe lik**ed** things from the Indies.

Did/Didn't

He **didn't** land in the Indies.

NEW VOCABULARY

across	get	near
after	gold	now
already	hope	order (v.)
America	hundreds	people
arrive	hundreds of	punish
back	thousands	sail
better	Indian	school
by	Indies	sell
call	island	ship (v.)
children	kill	slave
die	land	soon
discover	learn	Spain
enough	like	story
Europe	most	thing
European	Native	travel
far	American	way
find	native people	

GETTING READY

Introduce the past tense of regular verbs.

Write on the board:

hope	hoped
live	lived
want	wanted

a. Read each form of the verb and have students repeat chorally and individually.

b. Point out that "-ed" has three final sounds: [t], [d], and [ɪd].

PREVIEWING THE STORY

Have students talk about the story title and the picture to establish the context of the story. Ask some or all of the following questions:

Who do you think this is?
What do you know about Christopher Columbus?

READING THE STORY

1. Have students read the story silently.

2. **Check Reading Comprehension:** Ask students a question about each line of the story. For beginning-level students, ask these questions in the order below so that the questions follow the sequence of the story. For higher-level students, ask the questions in random order.

   When did Christopher Columbus sail from Spain?
   Where did he want to go?
   Why did Columbus want to go there?
   Before Columbus, how did Europeans travel to the Indies?
   What did Columbus hope to find?
   How did he want to get to the Indies?
   What ocean did he sail across?
   Did he land in the Indies?
   Where did he land?

   What do children often learn about Columbus in stories and in school?
   Did people already live in America before Columbus?
   What did Columbus call the native people?
   What do we call them today?
   Why did Columbus ship hundreds of native people to Spain?
   What happened to most of them?
   What did Columbus order them to find?
   What did he do if they didn't find enough gold?
   How many Indians died in the years after 1492?

3. Ask students if they have any questions about the story; check understanding of vocabulary.

4. **Choral Repetition:** Read aloud each line of the story and have students repeat.

5. **Class Circle Reading:** Have students read the story aloud as a class, with different students reading each line. (You can assign each line to a particular student or by seating patterns, or by letting students take turns spontaneously. In large classes, have a different group or row of students read each line.)

6. **Pair Practice:** Have students work in pairs, reading the passage to each other paragraph by paragraph. Circulate around the room and check students' reading and pronunciation, focusing more attention on students who need more assistance.

TEXT PAGES 101–102: *Check-Up*

VOCABULARY CHECK

1. Spain
2. the Indies
3. Atlantic
4. islands
5. Indians
6. gold

GRAMMAR CHECK

1. sailed
2. wanted
3. lived
4. landed
5. ordered

PRONUNCIATION PRACTICE

Have students practice saying the different sounds of the past tense *-ed* endings, chorally and individually.

PRONUNCIATION CHECK

Have students say each word and then write it in the correct column.

[t]	[d]	[ɪd]
shipped	discovered	landed
liked	called	wanted
hoped	died	
punished	traveled	
	sailed	
	lived	

After students fill in the words, have them practice saying the three sets of words chorally and individually.

MAPS, JOURNEYS, AND DISCOVERIES

1. Using a world map, have students trace Columbus's route. Then have students trace their own route to the United States.

2. Have students write about their routes and experiences during their journey to the United States. Publish a collection of student stories. Make copies for the school and for students to take home. (Or, if possible, put these stories on your school's website!)

3. Have students write a story about Columbus from the perspective of a native person in that time.

4. Have students discuss native people and explorers in their countries.

FOCUS

TOPIC

Colonization

GRAMMAR

Past Tense: Irregular Verbs

People from England first **came** to America
   in the 1600s.
They **grew** tobacco.

The first colony **was** in Jamestown, Virginia.
These people **were** called colonists.

NEW VOCABULARY

because	Pilgrim
colonist	Plymouth,
come	Massachusetts
England	religious
grow	ship
Jamestown, Virginia	tobacco
Mayflower	trade
original	

GETTING READY

1. Introduce the past tense of irregular verbs.

    Write on the board:

come	came
grow	grew
be	was/were

    Read the simple and past tense forms of the
    verbs. Have students repeat chorally and
    individually.

2. Bring in a map of the United States, and have
    students locate Virginia and Massachusetts.

PREVIEWING THE STORY

Have students talk about the story title and the
pictures to establish the context of the story. Ask
some or all of the following questions:

(Point to the first picture.)
What do you see in this picture?
Where do you think it is?
Who do you think lived there?

(Point to the second picture.)
Who are these people?
Where are they?
What are they doing?
What's wrong with the woman on the right?
Who is standing by the tree?

READING THE STORY

1. Have students read the story silently.

2. **Check Reading Comprehension:** Ask
    students a question about each line of the story.
    For beginning-level students, ask these questions
    in the order below so that the questions follow
    the sequence of the story. For higher-level
    students, ask the questions in random order.

    When did people from England first come to
       America?
    What were these people called?
    What were the original thirteen states called?

    Where was the first colony?
    When did the colonists come to Jamestown?
    What did the colonists in Jamestown do?

    When did colonists come to Plymouth,
       Massachusetts?
    What were these colonists called?
    Why did the Pilgrims come to America?
    What was the name of their ship?

3. Ask students if they have any questions about
    the story; check understanding of vocabulary.

4. **Choral Repetition:** Read aloud each line of the
    story and have students repeat.

5. **Class Circle Reading:** Have students read the
    story aloud as a class, with different students
    reading each line. (You can assign each line to a
    particular student or by seating patterns, or by
    letting students take turns spontaneously. In
    large classes, have a different group or row of
    students read each line.)

6. **Pair Practice:** Have students work in pairs,
    reading the passage to each other paragraph by
    paragraph. Circulate around the room and check
    students' reading and pronunciation, focusing
    more attention on students who need more
    assistance.

EXPANSION

Have students discuss the following:

a. Why do people come to the United States today?

b. Was/Is your native country a colony? Explain.

TEXT PAGES 104–105: *Check-Up*

VOCABULARY CHECK

1. England
2. colonies
3. colonists
4. Pilgrims
5. freedom
6. tobacco

DID YOU UNDERSTAND?

New Vocabulary: why

Have students answer these questions in full sentences.

1. The original thirteen states were called colonies.
2. The first American colony was in Jamestown, Virginia.
3. The Pilgrims came to Plymouth, Massachusetts, in 1620.
4. They wanted religious freedom.
5. The *Mayflower* was the name of the ship the Pilgrims sailed.
6. Colonists from England first came to Jamestown, Virginia, in 1607.

GRAMMAR CHECK

After students fill in the blanks with the correct forms of the verbs, have them work in pairs and practice asking and answering the questions.

1. come	3. came
came	came
2. grow	4. come
grew	came

LISTENING

Have students complete the exercises as you play the audio program or read the following:

Listen and circle the correct answer.

1. Where was the first American colony?
2. When did people from England come to the first American colony?
3. When did the Pilgrims come to America?
4. Why did the Pilgrims come to America?
5. What is the name of the colony that the Pilgrims came to?
6. What is the name of the ship that the Pilgrims sailed to America?

Answers

1. a	4. a
2. b	5. b
3. b	6. a

DISCUSSION

Lead a class discussion about the reasons people come to the United States today.

HOW ABOUT YOU?

Have students write the answers to these questions in the space provided. For additional speaking practice, students can discuss their answers.

INFORMATION EXCHANGE

Have the entire class practice asking the questions in the box. Then have students circulate around the room and interview five other students, writing the information they gather in the appropriate place on the grid. (For additional speaking practice, students can later report back to the class and tell about the students they interviewed.)

ANOTHER PERSPECTIVE

Have students look again at the picture at the bottom of page 103. Ask them to imagine that they are the Native American in that picture. Have them share their thoughts and feelings as the Pilgrims land in the place where they live.

TEXT PAGE 107: HOLIDAYS AND HISTORY: *Thanksgiving*

FOCUS

TOPIC

Colonization

GRAMMAR

Past Tense: Regular Verbs

The Native Americans help**ed** the Pilgrims.
The Pilgrims want**ed** to give thanks.

Many of them die**d** during the first year.
They celebrat**ed** a holiday.
They invit**ed** the Native Americans to a big dinner.

Past Tense: Irregular Verbs

Life **was** very difficult for the Pilgrims.
They **taught** the Pilgrims how to grow food.
The Native Americans **brought** most of the food.
The Native Americans already **had** celebrations like this one.

NEW VOCABULARY

bring	eat	potato
build	every	special
celebrate	fish (v.)	squash
celebration	food	teach
come together	fourth	thanks
corn	good	Thanksgiving
cranberry	holiday	turkey
difficult	house	usually
dinner	how to	
during	invite	

PREVIEWING THE STORY

Have students talk about the story title and the picture to establish the context of the story. Ask some or all of the following questions:

Who are these people?
Where are they?
When is this happening?
What are they doing?
What are they eating?
What are they wearing?
When do we celebrate Thanksgiving?

READING THE STORY

1. Have students read the story silently.

2. **Check Reading Comprehension:** Ask students a question about each line of the story. For beginning-level students, ask these questions in the order below so that the questions follow the sequence of the story. For higher-level students, ask the questions in random order.

> How was life for the Pilgrims in the Plymouth colony?
>
> What happened to many of them during the first year?
>
> Who helped the Pilgrims?
>
> What did the Native Americans teach the Pilgrims? (3 answers)
>
> Why did the Pilgrims want to give thanks?
>
> What did the Pilgrims celebrate?
>
> Who did the Pilgrims invite to their dinner?
>
> Who brought most of the food?
>
> What is this holiday in the Plymouth Colony called?
>
> Was it really the first Thanksgiving in America?
>
> Do Americans still celebrate Thanksgiving?
>
> When is Thanksgiving?
>
> What do families do on Thanksgiving?
>
> What do they usually eat?
>
> Why do Americans eat turkey, potatoes, corn, squash and cranberries on Thanksgiving?

3. Ask students if they have any questions about the story; check understanding of vocabulary.

4. **Choral Repetition:** Read aloud each line of the story and have students repeat.

5. **Class Circle Reading:** Have students read the story aloud as a class, with different students reading each line. (You can assign each line to a particular student or by seating patterns, or by letting students take turns spontaneously. In large classes, have a different group or row of students read each line.)

6. **Pair Practice:** Have students work in pairs, reading the passage to each other paragraph by paragraph. Circulate around the room and check students' reading and pronunciation, focusing more attention on students who need more assistance.

EXPANSION

1. Have students discuss:

> Do people in your native country celebrate a holiday like Thanksgiving?
>
> How do they celebrate?
>
> What do they eat?

2. Begin preparations for a Thanksgiving celebration in your classroom (the Civics Enrichment Project Activity on text page 116). Have students take responsibility for organizing the event, forming committees for different activities, and delegating tasks. (Students will prepare various dishes with Thanksgiving foods and share their recipe instructions with other students in conversation during the meal.

TEXT PAGES 108–109: *Check-Up*

VOCABULARY CHECK

> 1. helped
> 2. taught
> 3. celebrated
> 4. invited
> 5. came

DID YOU UNDERSTAND?

Have students answer these questions in full sentences.

> 1. The Native Americans helped the Pilgrims.
> 2. They taught the Pilgrims how to grow food, how to fish, and how to build houses.
> 3. They celebrated Thanksgiving.
> 4. They ate turkey, potatoes, corn, squash, and cranberries.

PRONUNCIATION CHECK

Have students say each word and then write it in the correct column.

[t]	[d]	[ɪd]
helped	sailed	invited
liked	died	celebrated

After students fill in the words, have them practice saying the three sets of words chorally and individually.

GRAMMAR CHECK

1. came
2. come
3. have
4. had
5. ate
6. eat

HOW ABOUT YOU?

Have students write the answers to these questions in the space provided. Then have students discuss their answers as a class or in small groups.

DISCUSSION

Lead a class discussion about students' adjustments to life in the United States.

TEXT PAGE 110: *The Thirteen Colonies*

FOCUS

TOPIC

Colonization

GRAMMAR

Past Tense: Irregular Verbs

The original thirteen states **were** called colonies.

NEW VOCABULARY

coast	Pennsylvania
	Delaware
New Hampshire	Maryland
Massachusetts	Virginia
Rhode Island	North Carolina
Connecticut	South Carolina
New York	Georgia
New Jersey	

GETTING READY

Bring in a map of the United States and point out the location of the first thirteen colonies.

PREVIEWING THE STORY

Have students talk about the story title and the illustration to establish the context of the story. Ask some or all of the following questions:

What is this a map of?
What part of the United States does this map show?
What states do you see?
What cities are on this map?

READING THE STORY

1. Have students read the story silently.
2. **Check Reading Comprehension:** Ask students a question about each line of the story. For beginning-level students, ask these questions in the order below so that the questions follow the sequence of the story. For higher-level students, ask the questions in random order.

What were the original thirteen states called? Where were these thirteen colonies?

What were the first thirteen colonies?

3. Ask students if they have any questions about the story; check understanding of vocabulary.

4. **Choral Repetition:** Read aloud each line of the story and have students repeat. (Read the names of the thirteen colonies one at a time, and have students repeat.)

5. **Class Circle Reading:** Have students read the story aloud as a class, with different students reading each line. (You can assign each line to a particular student or by seating patterns, or by letting students take turns spontaneously. In large classes, have a different group or row of students read each line. During this practice, have different students read each colony name as though it were a separate line.)

6. **Pair Practice:** Have students work in pairs, reading the passage to each other line by line. (Have students read each colony name as though it were a separate line.) Circulate around the room and check students' reading and pronunciation, focusing more attention on students who need more assistance.

TEXT PAGE 111: *Check-Up*

DID YOU UNDERSTAND?

Have students provide short answers to these questions.

1. Colonies.
2. Thirteen.
3. On the Atlantic Coast.

PRACTICING THE COLONIES

Connecticut	New York
Delaware	North Carolina
Georgia	Pennsylvania
Maryland	Rhode Island
Massachusetts	South Carolina
New Hampshire	Virginia
New Jersey	

QUESTIONS AND ANSWERS

This exercise offers students important practice with the multiple ways a question might be posed by the INS examiner. First, have students repeat each question after you. Then, have students practice asking and answering the questions with other students. Finally, have students write their answers to questions 1–4.

SOCIAL STUDIES ENRICHMENT

1. Have students compare the map on page 110 with a current map of the United States. See if they can figure out that mountain ranges served as the western boundaries of some colonies, explaining why the colonies were smaller in the colonial times.

2. Have students work in small groups, in pairs, or individually as they prepare an oral presentation about one of the original thirteen colonies. Have students give their presentations to the class.

TEXT PAGE 112: INTERVIEW:

Can You Name the Original Thirteen Colonies?

FOCUS

TOPIC

Colonization

GRAMMAR

Past Tense: Irregular Verbs

What **were** the original thirteen states called?

Did

What holiday **did** the American colonists celebrate?

FUNCTIONAL INTERVIEW SKILLS

Reporting Information
Giving Partial Answers to Difficult Questions
Hesitating

NEW VOCABULARY

a few	Go ahead.
now	I'm afraid . . .
remember	That's fine.
those	
time	

PRACTICING THE DIALOG

1. **Setting the Scene:** Have students look at the photo and determine who is talking: an INS examiner and an applicant. Establish the context: "The INS examiner is asking questions about the original thirteen colonies."

2. **Listening:** With books closed, have students listen to the dialog—presented by you, by a pair of students, or on the audio program.

3. **Choral Repetition:** With books still closed, model each line and have the whole class repeat in unison.

4. **Reading:** With books open, have students follow along as two students present the model dialog. Ask students if they have any questions and check understanding of vocabulary.

5. **Choral Conversation Practice:** Divide the class in half. Have Group 1 ask the questions and Group 2 give the answers; then reverse. (Or: You ask the questions and have the whole class answer in unison; then reverse.)

6. Call on one or two pairs of students to present the dialog, using the names of any four colonies.

7. **Pair Practice:** Have students practice the dialog in pairs, taking turns being the INS examiner and the applicant. Students should vary the names of the colonies, rather than repeating the ones used in the teacher's model.

8. Call on one or two more pairs of students to present the dialog to the class.

A. Now I want to ask you some questions about American history.
B. All right.
A. What were the original thirteen states called?
B. Let me see . . . They were called *colonies.*
A. And what holiday did the American colonists celebrate for the first time?
B. *Thanksgiving.*
A. That's right. And can you name the original thirteen colonies?
B. Hmm. I'm afraid I can't name all of them, but I can name a few.
A. Go ahead.
B. *(Colony), (colony), (colony), (colony) . . .* Those are the ones I remember.
A. That's fine.

---

86   CHAPTER 6

TEXT PAGE 113: SONG OF FREEDOM:

America (My Country 'Tis of Thee)

PRACTICING THE SONG

1. **Listening to the Lyrics:** Have students listen to the lyrics of the song by playing the audio or saying the lyrics yourself.

2. **Choral Repetition:** Read aloud each line of the song and have students repeat in unison.

3. **Listening to the Song:** Have students listen to the song by playing the audio or singing it yourself.

4. **Singing Aloud:** Play the instrumental version of the song and have students sing along. (The instrumental version follows the vocal version on the audio program.)

EXPANSION

Discuss with students the photos of the Macy's Thanksgiving Day parade, the Plimoth Plantation, and the Jamestown Settlement and the information in the caption for each photo.

TEXT PAGES 114–115: *Chapter Test*

You can use this test as a standardized form of assessment to measure student achievement of the curriculum objectives in Chapter 6. The test consists of 20 multiple-choice items and five sentences for dictation.

To score the test on a scale of 100:

- For each correct multiple-choice item, score four points.

- For each dictation sentence, do a general evaluation of the correctness of words, spelling, punctuation, and legibility. Score each sentence as follows:

   4 (Excellent), **3** (Good), **2** (Fair), **1** (Poor), **0** (Unsatisfactory)

Students can write their answers in the text or on the reproducible Chapter Test Answer Sheet provided in the Appendix.

A. DISCOVERY & COLONIZATION

1. D
2. B
3. B
4. C
5. A
6. D
7. A
8. D
9. D
10. C
11. A
12. C

B. GRAMMAR & VOCABULARY

13. B
14. C
15. D
16. B
17. C
18. B
19. A
20. C

C. DICTATION

Have students write these sentences as you read each sentence twice or play the audio program:

1. Columbus sailed to America in 1492.

2. The first American colony was in Virginia.

3. The Pilgrims came to America in 1620.

4. Thanksgiving is an American holiday in November.

5. The first thirteen (13) states were called colonies.

PERFORMANCE-BASED ASSESSMENT

These civics enrichment activities are designed to promote students' active participation in class and in the civic life of the community—through projects, issues discussions, community tasks, field trips, and Internet activities. Reproducible performance-based assessment forms for use in evaluating and documenting student participation in these activities are included in the Appendix.

CIVIC PARTICIPATION

Field Trip: Arrange for your class to visit a local supermarket. Have them talk with a supermarket employee about the products sold in the store. Have students look at the information that appears on the shelves, including unit prices, and have them learn how to compare prices of products or different sizes of the same product. Then have students talk with the manager of the supermarket. Have them tell about any foods they like that the supermarket doesn't have, and have them describe any problems they encounter when using a supermarket.

PROJECT ACTIVITY

Classroom Thanksgiving Celebration: Review with students the foods normally associated with the Thanksgiving holiday: turkey, potatoes, corn, squash, and cranberries. Have students prepare at home some dishes that use these foods – either native country recipes that use the Thanksgiving foods as ingredients, or recipes for typical American Thanksgiving dishes. If students wish to try making some typical American dishes, bring in cookbooks or prepare handouts with some recipes. (As an alternative to home preparation, if your class meets in a school that has a home economics classroom or other kitchen facilities, try to arrange permission for your class to use these facilities to prepare the foods.) During the holiday meal in class, have students share their recipe instructions. Have students take responsibility for all aspects of the holiday meal. Use the celebration as a basis for building students' skills in leadership and teamwork—key SCANS* skills useful for success in the workplace.

*Secretary's Commission on Achieving Necessary Skills

INTERNET ACTIVITY

Visiting the Plimoth Plantation colonial village: Have students go to the website listed in the text for Plimoth Plantation in Massachusetts. (This is the living history museum described in a photograph caption on text page 113.) Have them take the virtual tour and write sentences about what they see. Students can do this Internet activity individually, in pairs, or in small groups based on the computer resources available. Make sure students have the basic skills needed to access the Internet, such as using a computer keyboard and mouse and performing such tasks as clicking, scrolling, dragging, and typing URLs to access websites.

TECHNOLOGY ENRICHMENT

See Appendix page 160 for additional Internet enrichment activities related to this chapter.

<table>
<tr><td>

CHAPTER 7

</td><td>

OVERVIEW
Student Text
Pages 117–134

</td></tr>
</table>

TOPICS

The Revolutionary War
The Declaration of Independence

GRAMMAR

Past Tense: Regular Verbs
Past Tense: Irregular Verbs
Didn't

Review: To Be
Simple Present Tense

FUNCTIONAL INTERVIEW SKILLS

Asking for Clarification
Asking for Repetition
Reporting Information
Giving Alternative Information When Answers Aren't Known
Hesitating

KEY VOCABULARY

PEOPLE	PLACES	EVENTS	FUNCTIONAL EXPRESSIONS
colonist	America	band concert	All right.
family	Boston	barbecue	Could you please
friends	Boston Harbor	Boston Tea Party	say that again?
George Washington	colony	celebration	Did you say . . . ?
King of England	England	fireworks	Excuse me.
leader	Independence Hall	Fourth of July	Hmm.
Patrick Henry	Massachusetts	holiday	I don't understand.
representative	Philadelphia	Independence Day	I'm afraid I don't
Thomas Jefferson	United States	national holiday	know.
writer		parade	I'm sorry.
		picnic	
		Revolutionary War	

VERBS

begin	have
buy	like
carry	meet
celebrate	pay
complain	prepare
control	put
create	say
decide	sign
declare	take away
end	tell
fight	throw
form (v.)	vote
get together	want
give	win
go	write

OTHER WORDS

against	document	liberty
American	English	life
angry	equal	meeting
basic	famous	nobody
because	free	pursuit of
belief	goods	happiness
birthday	government	rights
city	high	ship
Colonial Army	history	tax
country	important	tea
death	independence	town
Declaration of	independent	war
Independence	law	water

RELATED PRACTICE

Foundations: Chapter 10
Word by Word Basic: pages 110–113
Word by Word: pages 66–67
Side by Side Book 1: Chapter 16
Side by Side Interactive CD-ROM / Side by Side TV Video: Level 1B, Segment 25
ExpressWays Book 1: Chapter 6

TEXT PAGE 117: *Vocabulary Preview*

You may want to introduce these words before beginning the chapter, or you may choose to wait until they first occur in a specific lesson. If you choose to introduce them at this point, here are some suggestions:

1. Have students look at the photographs on text page 117 and identify the words they already know.

2. Present the vocabulary. Say each word and have the class repeat it chorally and individually. Check students' understanding and pronunciation of the words.

3. Practice the vocabulary as a class, in pairs, or in small groups. Have students cover the word list and look at the photographs. Practice the words in the following ways:

   • Say a word or phrase and have students tell the number of the photograph.
   • Give the number of a photograph and have students say the word or phrase.

FOCUS

> ### TOPIC
> The Revolutionary War
>
> ### GRAMMAR
>
> **Past Tense: Regular Verbs**
>
> England want**ed** to control its colonies in
>   America.
> They decide**d** not to buy English goods.
>
> **Past Tense: Irregular Verbs**
>
> England **put** a high tax on tea.
> The colonists **were** very angry.
> Some colonists **went** onto a ship that
>   carried tea.
> The colonists **threw** the tea into the water.
> The colonists **met** in Philadelphia.
> They **wrote** to the King of England.
>
> **Didn't**
>
> The colonists in America **didn't** like this.
> The colonists **didn't** have any
>   representatives in England.

NEW VOCABULARY

against	English	prepare
angry	give	put
any	goods	tax
Boston	into	tea
Boston Tea	king	those
Party	liberty	throw
carry	meet	vote
complain	meeting	war
control	onto	water
death	pay	write
decide	Philadelphia	

PREVIEWING THE STORY

Have students talk about the story title and the
pictures to establish the context of the story. Ask
some or all of the following questions:

(Point to the picture on the left.)
Who are these people?
Where are they?
What do you think they're doing?
Why?

(Point to the picture on the right.)
Who are these people?
Where are they?
What do you think they're talking about?

READING THE STORY

1. Have students read the story silently.

2. **Check Reading Comprehension:** Ask
   students a question about each line of the story.
   For beginning-level students, ask these questions
   in the order below so that the questions follow
   the sequence of the story. For higher-level
   students, ask the questions in random order.

   > What country wanted to control its colonies in
   >   America?
   > How did the colonists in America feel about
   >   this?
   >
   > What did the colonists pay to England?
   > Did the colonists have representatives in
   >   England?
   > How did the colonists feel about English laws?
   >
   > What did England do in 1773?
   > How did the colonists feel about this?
   > What did some colonists in Boston do?
   > What did the colonists do with the tea?
   > What is this event called?
   >
   > Where did the colonists meet in 1774?
   > What did they decide?
   > Who did they write to? / What did they
   >   complain about?
   > Who said, "Give me liberty or give me death."?
   > What did the colonists prepare for?

3. Ask students if they have any questions about
   the story; check understanding of vocabulary.

4. **Choral Repetition:** Read aloud each line of the
   story and have students repeat.

5. **Class Circle Reading:** Have students read the
   story aloud as a class, with different students
   reading each line. (You can assign each line to a
   particular student or by seating patterns, or by
   letting students take turns spontaneously. In
   large classes, have a different group or row of
   students read each line.)

6. **Pair Practice:** Have students work in pairs, reading the passage to each other paragraph by paragraph. Circulate around the room and check students' reading and pronunciation, focusing more attention on students who need more assistance.

EXPANSION

Bring in a photo book about Boston that includes pictures of famous colonial sites, such as Faneuil Hall, Concord, and Lexington. Share it with students and discuss what they can see if they visit there.

TEXT PAGE 119: *Check-Up*

VOCABULARY CHECK

1. colonies
2. representatives
3. taxes
4. tea
5. liberty

DISCUSSION

Have students list the taxes they pay. Discuss how often these taxes are paid and what the money is used for. Have students list the different services students receive that are funded through tax revenue. (Point out that the colonists did not receive any services for their tax dollars.)

BOSTON TEA PARTY GRAMMAR CHECK

1. put
   put
2. go
   went
3. throw
   threw

TEXT PAGE 120: *The Revolutionary War*

FOCUS

TOPIC

The Revolutionary War

GRAMMAR

Past Tense: Regular Verbs

It end**ed** in 1783.
The colonists want**ed** to be independent.

Past Tense: Irregular Verbs

The Revolutionary War **began** in 1775.
The American colonies **fought** against England.
The colonies **won** the war.

Didn't

They **didn't** like English taxes.
The colonists **didn't** want England to control the colonies.

NEW VOCABULARY

begin	independent
Colonial Army	leader
end	Revolutionary War
fight	win

PREVIEWING THE STORY

Have students talk about the story title and the illustration to establish the context of the story. Ask some or all of the following questions:

Who are the people in this picture?
What are they doing?
Where are they?
What season is it? / How's the weather?
How do they feel?
Who is the man in the middle of the picture?
What are the men wearing?
What's going to happen?

READING THE STORY

1. Have students read the story silently.

2. **Check Reading Comprehension:** Ask students a question about each line of the story. For beginning-level students, ask these questions in the order below so that the questions follow the sequence of the story. For higher-level students, ask the questions in random order.

When did the Revolutionary War begin?
When did the Revolutionary War end?
Who did the American colonies fight against?

Why did the colonies fight the war?
What didn't the colonies want England to do?
What did the colonies want?

Who was the leader of the Colonial Army?
Who won the war?

3. Ask students if they have any questions about the story; check understanding of vocabulary.

4. **Choral Repetition:** Read aloud each line of the story and have students repeat.

5. **Class Circle Reading:** Have students read the story aloud as a class, with different students reading each line. (You can assign each line to a particular student or by seating patterns, or by letting students take turns spontaneously. In large classes, have a different group or row of students read each line.)

6. **Pair Practice:** Have students work in pairs, reading the passage to each other paragraph by paragraph. Circulate around the room and check students' reading and pronunciation, focusing more attention on students who need more assistance.

EXPANSION

1. Discuss revolutions and revolutionary heroes in students' native countries.

2. Have students prepare a short report about George Washington.

3. Locate sites of important Revolutionary War battles on a map of the United States.

TEXT PAGE 121: *Check-Up*

GRAMMAR CHECK

After students fill in the blanks with the correct forms of the verbs, have them work in pairs and practice asking and answering the questions.

1. begin
   began

2. fight
   fought

3. win
   won

DID YOU UNDERSTAND?

Have students answer these questions in full sentences.

1. We fought England during the Revolutionary War.
2. They didn't like English taxes. / They didn't like English laws. / They didn't have any representatives in England.
3. George Washington was the leader of the colonists' army.
4. Patrick Henry said, "Give me liberty or give me death."

FOCUS

TOPIC

The Revolutionary War

GRAMMAR

Past Tense: Regular Verbs

The colonists want**ed** to be independent.
Representatives sign**ed** the Declaration of
Independence.

Past Tense: Irregular Verbs

The Revolutionary War **began** in 1775.
The colonists **met** at Independence Hall in
Philadelphia.
Thomas Jefferson **wrote** the Declaration of
Independence.

Didn't

The American colonists **didn't** want England
to control the colonies.

NEW VOCABULARY

Declaration of	Independence Hall
Independence	sign
declare	their
free	

PREVIEWING THE STORY

Have students talk about the story title and the
illustration to establish the context of the story. Ask
some or all of the following questions:

Who are the people in the picture?
Where are they?
What are they doing?
What's the man with the pen signing?

READING THE STORY

1. Have students read the story silently.

2. **Check Reading Comprehension:** Ask
students a question about each line of the story.
For beginning-level students, ask these questions
in the order below so that the questions follow
the sequence of the story. For higher-level
students, ask the questions in random order.

   What didn't the American colonies want
      England to do?
   What did the colonists want?
   Who did the colonists want to be
      independent of?

   When did the Revolutionary War begin?
   Where did the colonists meet in 1776?
   What did they decide to declare?
   Who wrote the Declaration of Independence?
   What did the Declaration of Independence
      say?
   When did they sign the Declaration of
      Independence?

3. Ask students if they have any questions about
the story; check understanding of vocabulary.

4. **Choral Repetition:** Read aloud each line of the
story and have students repeat.

5. **Class Circle Reading:** Have students read the
story aloud as a class, with different students
reading each line. (You can assign each line to a
particular student or by seating patterns, or by
letting students take turns spontaneously. In
large classes, have a different group or row of
students read each line.)

6. **Pair Practice:** Have students work in pairs,
reading the passage to each other paragraph by
paragraph. Circulate around the room and check
students' reading and pronunciation, focusing
more attention on students who need more
assistance.

GRAMMAR CHECK

After students fill in the blanks with the correct forms of the verbs, have them work in pairs and practice asking and answering the questions.

1. meet
   met
2. write
   wrote
3. say
   said

QUESTIONS AND ANSWERS

This exercise offers students important practice with the multiple ways a question might be posed by the INS examiner. First, have students repeat each question after you. Then, have students practice asking and answering the questions with other students. Finally, have students write their answers to questions 1 and 2.

1. Thomas Jefferson.
2. On July 4, 1776.

TEXT PAGES 124: DOCUMENT OF FREEDOM:
The Declaration of Independence

FOCUS

TOPIC

The Declaration of Independence

GRAMMAR

Past Tense: Regular Verbs

The thirteen colonies declar**ed** their
  independence.
They sign**ed** the Declaration of
  Independence on July 4, 1776.

NEW VOCABULARY

base	must
basic	nobody
belief	take away
create	
equal	life, liberty, and the
form (v.)	pursuit of happiness
man	

PREVIEWING THE STORY

Have students talk about the story title and the illustration to establish the context of the story. Ask some or all of the following questions:

What is a document?
What do you think *Document of Freedom* means?
What is the date on this document?
What is at the bottom of the document?
  (Signatures)

READING THE STORY

1. Have students read the story silently.

2. **Check Reading Comprehension:** Ask students a question about each line of the story. For beginning-level students, ask these questions in the order below so that the questions follow the sequence of the story. For higher-level students, ask the questions in random order.

   What is the Declaration of Independence?
   What does the Declaration of Independence say?
   What is the basic belief of the Declaration of Independence?
   What do people have that nobody can take away?
   What are the rights that nobody can take away?

According to the Declaration of Independence, who can tell the government what to do?

What must the government do?

What can the people do if they want to?

What did the colonies do based on these beliefs?

When did they sign the Declaration of Independence?

3. Ask students if they have any questions about the story; check understanding of vocabulary.

4. **Choral Repetition:** Read aloud each line of the story and have students repeat.

5. **Class Circle Reading:** Have students read the story aloud as a class, with different students reading each line. (You can assign each line to a particular student or by seating patterns, or by letting students take turns spontaneously. In large classes, have a different group or row of students read each line.)

6. **Pair Practice:** Have students work in pairs, reading the passage to each other paragraph by paragraph. Circulate around the room and check students' reading and pronunciation, focusing more attention on students who need more assistance.

EXPANSION

1. Have students look again at the illustration on page 124. Ask them what they see at the bottom of the Declaration of Independence. (Signatures.) Ask them whose signature is the largest. (John Hancock.) Explain that this is a very famous signature. Hancock signed his name very large so that the King of England could see it without his glasses. Even today the expression "put your John Hancock on this" is used to mean writing one's signature.

2. Bring in a copy of the Declaration of Independence. Affix some additional paper at the bottom and have all the students sign their names underneath the colonists' signatures. Display the Declaration of Independence on a bulletin board in your classroom.

TEXT PAGE 125: *Check-Up*

VOCABULARY CHECK

1. document
2. belief
3. government
4. liberty
5. independence

LISTENING

Have students complete the exercises as you play the audio program or read the following:

Listen and circle the correct answer.

1. When did the colonists sign the Declaration of Independence?
2. Where did the colonists sign the Declaration of Independence?
3. Why did the colonists sign the Declaration of Independence?
4. Who did the colonies fight against during the Revolutionary War?
5. When did the colonies fight the Revolutionary War?
6. Why did the colonies fight the Revolutionary War?

Answers

1. b	4. a
2. a	5. b
3. c	6. c

HOW ABOUT YOU?

Have students discuss these questions in pairs, in small groups, or as a class. If working in pairs or groups, students should report what they have discussed to the entire class.

TEXT PAGE 126: VOICE OF FREEDOM: *Thomas Jefferson*

(As noted in the text, this lesson is provided for enrichment and speaking practice. It is not required for the INS interview.)

FOCUS

> ### TOPIC
>
> The Declaration of Independence
>
> ### GRAMMAR
>
> **Past Tense: Regular Verbs**
>
> The thirteen colonies sign**ed** the Declaration of Independence.
>
> **Past Tense: Irregular Verbs**
>
> Thomas Jefferson **wrote** the Declaration of Independence.

NEW VOCABULARY

> beautiful
> famous
> word

GETTING READY

Ask students to identify the person whose face is on a nickel and a two-dollar bill (if you can find one).

PREVIEWING THE STORY

Have students talk about the story title and the pictures to establish the context of the story. Ask some or all of the following questions:

> (Point to the first picture.)
> Where have you seen this face before?
> Who was Thomas Jefferson?
> What did he do?
>
> (Point to the second picture.)
> What is the name of this building?
> (Hint: This is the outside of the building you
>   see in the picture on page 122.)
> Where is this building?
> What happened here?

READING THE STORY

1. Have students first read the introductory sentences silently.

2. **Check Reading Comprehension:** Ask students questions about the introduction.

   > Who wrote the Declaration of Independence?
   > Where did the thirteen colonies sign the
   >   Declaration of Independence?
   > When?

3. **Listening:** With books closed, have students listen to the introduction and excerpt in the box—presented by you or on the audio program.

4. **Reading:** Have students read along silently as they listen to the passage again—presented by you or on the audio program.

5. **Choral Reading:** Have students read the passage aloud in unison, along with you or the audio program.

6. Ask students if they understand the general meaning of the passage. (They do not need to know the exact meaning of unfamiliar words.)

7. **Public Speaking Practice:** Have individual students present the excerpted passages to the class. If you feel it is appropriate to do so, help students with their diction and projection to improve their public speaking skills in English.

8. **Pair Practice:** Have students work in pairs, taking turns reading the passage to each other. Circulate around the room and check students' reading and pronunciation, focusing more attention on students who need more assistance.

EXPANSION

1. Bring in a photo book about Independence Hall. Share it with students and discuss what they can see if they visit there.

2. Have students prepare short oral or written reports about Thomas Jefferson. Ask them to include the following information:

   > When was he born?
   > Where was he born?
   > Where did he live?
   > What did he do?
   > When was he President?
   > When did he die?

3. Have an oratorical contest. Have interested students memorize the excerpt from the Declaration of Independence and present it to the class. Have class members vote on the best rendition, and award a prize to the winner.

TEXT PAGE 127: INTERVIEW: *Did You Say When or Where?*

FOCUS

TOPIC

The Declaration of Independence

GRAMMAR

Past Tense

Where **did** the colonists sign the Declaration of Independence?
Did you say when or where?

FUNCTIONAL INTERVIEW SKILLS

Asking for Clarification
Reporting Information

NEW VOCABULARY

---

adopt

PRACTICING THE DIALOGS

There are two dialogs. Follow these steps for the first dialog, and then go on to the second dialog.

1. **Setting the Scene:** Have students look at the photo and determine who is talking: an INS examiner and an applicant. Establish the context: "The INS examiner is asking questions about the Declaration of Independence."

2. **Listening:** With books closed, have students listen to the dialog—presented by you, by a pair of students, or on the audio program.

3. **Choral Repetition:** With books still closed, model each line and have the whole class repeat in unison.

4. **Reading:** With books open, have students follow along as two students present the model dialog. Ask students if they have any questions and check understanding of vocabulary.

5. **Choral Conversation Practice:** Divide the class in half. Have Group 1 ask the questions and Group 2 give the answers; then reverse. (Or: You ask the questions and have the whole class answer in unison; then reverse.)

6. Call on one or two pairs of students to present the model dialog.

7. **Pair Practice:** Have students practice the dialog in pairs, taking turns being the INS examiner and the applicant.

8. Call on one or two more pairs of students to present the dialog to the class.

A. Where did the colonists sign the Declaration of Independence?
B. Excuse me. Did you say when or where?
A. Where?
B. At *Independence Hall* in *Philadelphia.*

A. When was the Declaration of Independence adopted?
B. Excuse me. Did you say when or where?
A. When?
B. On *July 4, 1776.*

TEXT PAGE 128: HOLIDAYS AND HISTORY:
Independence Day (The Fourth of July)

FOCUS

TOPIC

Independence Day (The Fourth of July)

GRAMMAR

To Be (Review)

Independence Day **is** a very happy celebration.
There **are** parades and band concerts.

Simple Present Tense (Review)

Americans **celebrate** a national holiday.
Many Americans **get** together with family
    and friends.

Past Tense: Regular Verbs

On July 4, 1776 the thirteen colonies
    declare**d** their independence.

NEW VOCABULARY

band concert	national holiday
barbecue	outside
birthday	parade
fireworks	picnic
happy	summer

PREVIEWING THE STORY

Have students talk about the story title and the
photographs to establish the context of the story.
Ask some or all of the following questions:

(Point to the first picture.)
What are these people doing?
Why?
What are they carrying?

(Point to the second picture.)
What is this a picture of?
When have you seen fireworks in the U.S.?
Do you ever have fireworks in your native
    country? When?

READING THE STORY

1. Have students read the story silently.
2. **Check Reading Comprehension:** Ask
students a question about each line of the story.
For beginning-level students, ask these questions
in the order below, so that the questions follow
the sequence of the story. For higher-level
students, ask the questions in random order.

    What do Americans celebrate on July 4th?
    What is the holiday called?
    What's another name for Independence Day?
    What do Americans celebrate on this day?
    Why is it the country's birthday?

    What kind of celebration is Independence Day?
    What do many Americans do on that day?
    How do many Americans celebrate outside on
        that day?
    What happens in many cities and towns on
        Independence Day?

3. Ask students if they have any questions about
the story; check understanding of vocabulary.
4. **Choral Repetition:** Read aloud each line of the
story and have students repeat.
5. **Class Circle Reading:** Have students read the
story aloud as a class, with different students
reading each line. (You can assign each line to a
particular student or by seating patterns, or by
letting students take turns spontaneously. In
large classes, have a different group or row of
students read each line.)
6. **Pair Practice:** Have students work in pairs,
reading the passage to each other paragraph by
paragraph. Circulate around the room and check
students' reading and pronunciation, focusing more
attention on students who need more assistance.

DISCUSSION

Have students discuss their answers to the
questions in the final paragraph. Have them
discuss how they celebrate Independence Day in the
United States. Also have them discuss any
celebrations like Independence Day in their native
countries. Have them describe how people celebrate
these holidays.

EXPANSION

Have a Fourth of July picnic celebration with your class (even if it isn't the Fourth of July)! Prepare typical foods (hot dogs, hamburgers, corn on the cob, etc.), play some John Philip Sousa marches as patriotic background music, and if an outdoor picnic is possible, do some typical activities, such as a softball game, a three-legged race, a pie-eating contest, or simply toss a frisbee around and have some fun. (Encourage students to wear red, white, and blue clothing to help set the mood.)

TEXT PAGE 129: INTERVIEW: *Could You Please Say That Again?*

FOCUS

TOPIC The Declaration of Independence **GRAMMAR** **Didn't** I **didn't** understand. **FUNCTIONAL INTERVIEW SKILLS** Asking for Repetition Reporting Information

NEW VOCABULARY

main writer

PRACTICING THE DIALOGS

There are two dialogs. Follow these steps for the first dialog, and then go on to the second dialog.

1. **Setting the Scene:** Have students look at the photo and determine who is talking: an INS examiner and an applicant. Establish the context: "The INS examiner is asking questions about the Declaration of Independence."

2. **Listening:** With books closed, have students listen to the dialog—presented by you, by a pair of students, or on the audio program.

3. **Choral Repetition:** With books still closed, model each line and have the whole class repeat in unison.

4. **Reading:** With books open, have students follow along as two students present the model dialog. Ask students if they have any questions and check understanding of vocabulary.

5. **Choral Conversation Practice:** Divide the class in half. Have Group 1 ask the questions and Group 2 give the answers; then reverse. (Or: You ask the questions and have the whole class answer in unison; then reverse.)

6. Call on one or two pairs of students to present the model dialog.

7. **Pair Practice:** Have students practice the dialog in pairs, taking turns being the INS examiner and the applicant.

8. Call on one or two more pairs of students to present the dialog to the class.

A. Who was the main writer of the Declaration of Independence? B. I'm sorry. I didn't understand. Could you please say that again? A. Who wrote the Declaration of Independence? B. *Thomas Jefferson.* A. What is the basic belief of the Declaration of Independence? B. I'm sorry. I didn't understand. Could you please say that again? A. What does the Declaration of Independence say? B. It says that *all men are created equal.*

FOCUS

TOPIC

The Declaration of Independence

GRAMMAR

Past Tense: Regular Verbs

How many people sign**ed** the Declaration of Independence?

Past Tense: Irregular Verbs

Do you know what country we **fought** during the Revolutionary War?

FUNCTIONAL INTERVIEW SKILLS

Reporting Information
Hesitating
Giving Alternative Information When
    Answers Aren't Known

NEW VOCABULARY

but

PRACTICING THE DIALOG

1. **Setting the Scene:** Have students look at the photo and determine who is talking: an INS examiner and an applicant. Establish the context: "The INS examiner is asking questions about the Declaration of Independence."

2. **Listening:** With books closed, have students listen to the dialog—presented by you, by a pair of students, or on the audio program.

3. **Choral Repetition:** With books still closed, model each line and have the whole class repeat in unison.

4. **Reading:** With books open, have students follow along as two students present the model dialog. Ask students if they have any questions and check understanding of vocabulary.

5. **Choral Conversation Practice:** Divide the class in half. Have Group 1 ask the questions and Group 2 give the answers; then reverse. (Or: You ask the questions and have the whole class answer in unison; then reverse.)

6. Call on one or two pairs of students to present the dialog.

7. **Pair Practice:** Have students practice the dialog in pairs, taking turns being the INS examiner and the applicant.

8. Call on one or two more pairs of students to present the dialog to the class.

Dialog Notes

Line 7: Be sure to point out to students that, for the INS interview, they are not officially required to know how many people signed the Declaration of Independence. The question appears in this dialog to give students practice dealing with a very difficult and, in this case, inappropriate question.

Line 8: Point out to students that while the applicant may not know the answer to the examiner's question, the applicant offers some other information instead. ("I'm afraid I don't know. But I know that Thomas Jefferson wrote it.") By doing this, the applicant demonstrates that he has studied about the subject and indeed knows some information about the subject. This is a very important functional interview skill students need in order to deal with difficult or inappropriate questions.

Line 9: ("Can you tell me anything else about the Declaration of Independence?") The examiner is trying to be helpful by asking the applicant to tell her anything at all about the Declaration of Independence. However, this question is actually very difficult since it does not ask for any specific information and therefore doesn't guide the student toward providing any particular information. Students therefore need practice responding to such nonspecific questions.

A. Now I want to ask you some questions about the American Revolution.
B. All right.
A. Do you know what country we fought during the Revolutionary War?
B. Yes. It was *England*.
A. And can you tell me who the leader of the Colonial Army was?
B. Yes. It was *George Washington*.
A. How many people signed the Declaration of Independence?
B. Hmm. I'm afraid I don't know. But I know that *Thomas Jefferson* wrote it.

A. That's right. Can you tell me anything else about the Declaration of Independence?
B. Yes. *It says that all men are created equal. / The colonies signed it on July 4, 1776. / The colonies signed it at Independence Hall in Philadelphia. / etc.*
A. Very good.

TEXT PAGE 131: *Review*

TALKING TIME LINE: Important Dates in U.S. History

Have students complete the time line. Then have them work in pairs, asking and answering the questions at the bottom of the page, based on the information recorded on the time line.

1492	Columbus sailed to America.
1607	Colonists came to Jamestown, Virginia.
1620	Pilgrims came to the Plymouth Colony.
1775	The Revolutionary War began.
1776	The colonies declared their independence.
1783	The Revolutionary War ended.

TEXT PAGES 132–133: *Chapter Test*

You can use this test as a standardized form of assessment to measure student achievement of the curriculum objectives in Chapter 7. The test consists of 20 multiple-choice items and five sentences for dictation.

To score the test on a scale of 100:

- For each correct multiple-choice item, score four points.

- For each dictation sentence, do a general evaluation of the correctness of words, spelling, punctuation, and legibility. Score each sentence as follows:

  4 (Excellent), **3** (Good), **2** (Fair), **1** (Poor), **0** (Unsatisfactory)

Students can write their answers in the text or on the reproducible Chapter Test Answer Sheet provided in the Appendix.

A. COMPLETE THE SENTENCES

1. C
2. C
3. A
4. D
5. D
6. C
7. A
8. B
9. C
10. B
11. C
12. B

B. ANSWER THE QUESTIONS

13. A
14. D
15. B
16. B
17. C
18. A
19. D
20. D

C. DICTATION

Have students write these sentences as you read each sentence twice or play the audio program:

1. The colonists didn't like English laws.

2. Thomas Jefferson wrote the Declaration of Independence.

3. The colonies signed the Declaration of Independence in 1776.

4. The Fourth (4th) of July is America's birthday.

5. Independence Day is a summer holiday.

TEXT PAGE 134: *Civics Enrichment*

PERFORMANCE-BASED ASSESSMENT

These civics enrichment activities are designed to promote students' active participation in class and in the civic life of the community—through projects, issues discussions, community tasks, field trips, and Internet activities. Reproducible performance-based assessment forms for use in evaluating and documenting student participation in these activities are included in the Appendix.

CIVIC PARTICIPATION

Have students brainstorm the kinds of taxes people pay to your local government, such as sales taxes, real estate taxes, and taxes on cars or other personal property. Have them discuss what the local government does with this money by brainstorming a list of all the services provided to the community. Then have students obtain information from your city hall, town hall, or other local government office about local government services and their costs. As a class, students should make a chart that shows the services and how much they cost. Have students take responsibility for all aspects of this activity, including obtaining the information and designing the chart of government services and costs. Use the activity as a basis for building students' skills in leadership, teamwork, and acquiring, evaluating, and communicating information—key SCANS* skills useful for success in the workplace.

PROJECT ACTIVITY

Time Line Bulletin Board Project: In this project, students make a large time line on a bulletin board. On the time line, they show events that happened in

the history of their countries and events in U.S. history that they studied in the chapter. Students should draw pictures of the events and write brief paragraphs about them to include on the bulletin board. Have students take responsibility for all aspects of this project. Have them identify the particular tasks involved in the project, who will accomplish each task, what resources are needed, and what form the final bulletin board display will take. Use the project as a basis for building students' skills in leadership, teamwork, and communicating information—key SCANS* skills useful for success in the workplace.

INTERNET ACTIVITY

Visiting historic Philadelphia online: Have students go to the website listed in the text for the Independence Hall Association. Have them take the virtual tour, or have them click on the following places in the Index: Betsy Ross House, First Bank of the United States, Independence Hall, and Liberty Bell. Have students write sentences about what they see and why these places are important in U.S. history. Students can do this Internet activity individually, in pairs, or in small groups based on the computer resources available. Make sure students have the basic skills needed to access the Internet, such as using a computer keyboard and mouse and performing such tasks as clicking, scrolling, dragging, and typing URLs to access websites.

TECHNOLOGY ENRICHMENT

See Appendix page 160 for additional Internet enrichment activities related to this chapter.

*Secretary's Commission on Achieving Necessary Skills

<table>
<tr>
<td>

CHAPTER
8

</td>
<td>

OVERVIEW
Student Text
Pages 135–152

</td>
</tr>
</table>

TOPICS

The Constitution
Branches of Government
The Bill of Rights
George Washington

GRAMMAR

Past Tense: Regular and Irregular Verbs
Past Tense: Was/Were
Present Tense Review

FUNCTIONAL INTERVIEW SKILLS

Reporting Information
Handling Not Knowing an Answer
Indicating Understanding
Hesitating

KEY VOCABULARY

PEOPLE
Cabinet
chief executive
citizen
Commander-in-Chief
George Washington
leader
member
natural-born citizen
non-citizen
person
police
President
representative
senator
Speaker of the House
   of Representatives
Supreme Court justice
Vice President

PLACES
America
colony
Philadelphia
U.S. Capitol
United States

**BRANCHES OF
GOVERNMENT**
Congress
executive branch
federal courts
House of
   Representatives
judicial branch
legislative branch
Senate
Supreme Court

FUNCTIONAL EXPRESSIONS
All right.
I'm afraid I don't remember.
Let me see.
That's correct.

THE CONSTITUTION & BILL OF RIGHTS
Constitution
Constitutional Convention
document
First Amendment
freedom of assembly
freedom of religion
freedom of speech
freedom of the press

freedoms
introduction
Preamble
rights
supreme law of the
   land
system of government
We the People

VERBS		**OTHER WORDS**	
accuse	go to court	age	lawyer
advise	guarantee	American history	life
appoint	have	armed forces	magnificent
approve	inaugurate	bill	national
become	live	Colonial Army	powers
begin	make the laws	court	requirement
change	meet	crime	Revolutionary War
declare war	respect	excellent	rule
describe	serve	form	separate
die	sign	free	special
enforce the laws	vote	government	state
establish	win	important	strong
explain the laws	work	independent	term
give	write	law	trial

RELATED PRACTICE

Foundations: Chapter 11
Word by Word Basic: pages 114–127
Word by Word: pages 68–74
Side by Side Book 1: Chapter 17
Side by Side Interactive CD-ROM / Side by Side TV Video: Level 1B, Segment 26
ExpressWays Book 1: Chapter 7

TEXT PAGE 135: *Vocabulary Preview*

You may want to introduce these words before beginning the chapter, or you may choose to wait until they first occur in a specific lesson. If you choose to introduce them at this point, here are some suggestions:

1. Have students look at the photographs on text page 135 and identify the words they already know.

2. Present the vocabulary. Say each word and have the class repeat it chorally and individually. Check students' understanding and pronunciation of the words.

3. Practice the vocabulary as a class, in pairs, or in small groups. Have students cover the word list and look at the photographs. Practice the words in the following ways:

   • Say a phrase and have students tell the number of the photograph.
   • Give the number of a photograph and have students say the phrase.

FOCUS

> **TOPIC**
>
> The Constitution
>
> **GRAMMAR**
>
> **Past Tense: Regular and Irregular Verbs**
>
> The Constitution establish**ed** the form of government in the United States.
> It describ**ed** the powers of the national government.
>
> The colonies in America **won** the Revolutionary War in 1783.
> But they **had** a problem.
> Representatives from the states **met** in Philadelphia.
>
> **Past Tense: Was/Were**
>
> There **wasn't** one strong national government.
> They **were** free and independent states.
>
> **Present Tense**
>
> It **is** the supreme law of the land.

NEW VOCABULARY

describe	problem
establish	separate
power	strong

PREVIEWING THE STORY

Have students talk about the story title and the illustration to establish the context of the story. Ask some or all of the following questions:

Who are these people?
Who is the man in the center?
What are they doing?
Where are they?
What is a constitution?
Does your native country have a constitution?
What does it say?

READING THE STORY

1. Have students read the story silently.

2. **Check Reading Comprehension:** Ask students a question about each line of the story. For beginning-level students, ask these questions in the order below so that the questions follow the sequence of the story. For higher-level students, ask the questions in random order.

   Who won the Revolutionary War? When?
   What did the colonies become?
   What problem did the colonies have?
   How many governments did the thirteen states have?
   Was there one strong national government?

   What happened in Philadelphia in 1787?
   What did they write?

   What did the Constitution establish?
   What are the three branches of government?
   What did the Constitution describe?

   What is the highest law in the United States?
   What is the supreme law of the land?

3. Ask students if they have any questions about the story; check understanding of vocabulary.

4. **Class Circle Reading:** Have students read the story aloud as a class, with different students reading each line. (You can assign each line to a particular student or by seating patterns, or by letting students take turns spontaneously. In large classes, have a different group or row of students read each line.)

5. **Pair Practice:** Have students work in pairs, reading the passage to each other paragraph by paragraph. Circulate around the room and check students' reading and pronunciation, focusing more attention on students who need more assistance.

EXPANSION

1. Bring in a copy of the Constitution. Show students the various articles of the Constitution and describe what the articles are about.

2. Have a "Constitutional Convention" in class. Have students write a constitution for the class or the school. Have them decide who should have which powers and responsibilities.

TEXT PAGE 137: *Check-Up*

VOCABULARY CHECK

1. colonies
2. Constitution
3. branches
4. powers
5. supreme

GRAMMAR CHECK

1. were
2. weren't
3. was
4. wasn't
5. were

QUESTIONS AND ANSWERS

This exercise offers students important practice with the multiple ways a question might be posed by the INS examiner. First, have students repeat each question after you. Then, have students practice asking and answering the questions with other students. Finally, have students write their answers to questions 1 and 2.

1. The Constitution.
2. In 1787.

DISCUSSION

Have students describe their native country's constitution.

TEXT PAGES 138–140: *Three Branches of Government*

FOCUS

TOPIC

Branches of Government

GRAMMAR

Past Tense: Regular and Irregular Verbs

The Constitution establish**ed** three branches of government.
The Constitution **gave** the rules for the three branches of government.

Present Tense

The states **have** different numbers of representatives.
The legislative branch **makes** the laws of the United States.

A senator's term **is** six years.
There **are** one hundred senators in the Senate.

NEW VOCABULARY

advise	inaugurate
age	member
at least	natural born citizen
before	old(er)
bill	requirement
Cabinet	Speaker of the House
certain	of Representatives

PREVIEWING THE STORY

(This reading passage has four sections, each introduced by one or more photographs. You may want to treat each section as a separate story, previewing and reading one section before going on to the next.)

Have students talk about the story title and the photographs to establish the context of the story. Ask some or all of the following questions:

(Point to the photograph on page 138.)
Who are these people?
Where are they?
How many people do you think there are in the photograph?
What are they doing?

(Point to the photographs on page 139.)
What is this building?
Who lives/works there?
Where is it?

Who is this man?
What does he do?
Where does he live?

(Point to the photograph at the top of page 140.)
Who is this man?
Who is the woman standing next to him?
What is he doing?
Why? What happened?
Where are these people in this photograph?
When did this happen?

(Point to the photographs at the bottom of page 140.)
What building is this?
Where is it located?
Who works there?

Who are these people?
What do they do?

READING THE STORY

1. Have students read the story silently.

2. **Check Reading Comprehension:** Ask students a question about each line of the story. For beginning-level students, ask these questions in the order below, so that the questions follow the sequence of the story. For higher-level students, ask the questions in random order.

   Page 138:

   How many branches of government did the Constitution establish? What are they?

   What does the legislative branch do?
   What is the legislative branch called?
   What are the two parts of Congress?
   Where does the Congress meet?

   How many senators are there?
   How many senators are there from each state?
   How long is a senator's term?

   How many representatives are there?
   How many representatives does each state have?
   Which states have more representatives?
   Which states have fewer representatives?
   How long is a representative's term?

   What document gives powers to the Congress?
   Name one important power of Congress.

Page 139:

What does the executive branch do?
Who works in the executive branch?
Who is the chief executive of the United States?
Who is the Commander-in-Chief of the armed forces?

What does the President sign?
Who does the President appoint?
What does the Cabinet do?

Can anybody become President?
What kind of citizen must the President be?
How old must the President be?
How long must the President live in the United States before becoming President?

Page 140 (top):

How long is the President's term?
How many terms can the President serve?
When do Americans vote for the President?
When is the President inaugurated?

Who becomes President if the President dies?
Who becomes President if both the President and Vice President die?

Page 140 (bottom):

What does the judicial branch do?
What is the judicial branch?
What is the highest court in the United States?
How many Supreme Court justices are there?
Who appoints them? Who approves them?
How long do they serve?

3. Ask students if they have any questions about the story; check understanding of vocabulary.

4. **Class Circle Reading:** Have students read the story aloud as a class, with different students reading each line. (You can assign each line to a particular student or by seating patterns, or by letting students take turns spontaneously. In large classes, have a different group or row of students read each line.)

5. **Pair Practice:** Have students work in pairs, reading the passage to each other paragraph by paragraph. Circulate around the room and check students' reading and pronunciation, focusing more attention on students who need more assistance.

DID YOU UNDERSTAND?

Have students provide short answers to these questions. Then, have students practice these questions conversationally.

1. The legislative branch.
2. The judicial branch.
3. The executive branch.
4. 100.
5. 435.
6. (Answers vary.)
7. In the U.S. Capitol.
8. The President.
9. The President.
10. Must be a natural born citizen./Must be age 35 or older./Must live in the U.S. at least 14 years.
11. The Cabinet.
12. The Speaker of the House of Representatives.
13. The Supreme Court.
14. Nine.
15. The President.
16. 6 years.
17. 2 years.
18. November.
19. January.
20. There are two from each state.

YOUR GOVERNMENT OFFICIALS

Have students write the names of the government officials listed in this exercise.

QUESTIONS AND ANSWERS

This exercise offers students important practice with the multiple ways a question might be posed by the INS examiner. First, have students repeat each question after you. Then, have students practice asking and answering the questions with other students. For additional practice, students can write their answers to the questions on a separate sheet of paper.

DISCUSSION

Have students bring in and discuss photographs or articles from newspapers or magazines that depict current activities of the President, Vice President, members of Congress, and Supreme Court justices.

TEXT PAGES 143: DOCUMENT OF FREEDOM:

The Preamble to the Constitution

(As noted in the text, this lesson is provided for enrichment and speaking practice. It is not required for the INS interview.)

FOCUS

TOPIC

The Constitution

GRAMMAR

Present Tense: Review

The Constitution of the United States **is** a magnificent document.
We **have** the same system of government today.
The Preamble begin**s** with three very famous words.

NEW VOCABULARY

introduction
magnificent
Preamble
system
We the People . . .

PREVIEWING THE STORY

Have students talk about the story title and graphic to establish the context of the story. Ask some or all of the following questions:

What do these words say?
Where can you find them?
What is the Constitution?
What is a preamble?

READING THE STORY

1. Have students first read the introductory sentences silently.

2. **Check Reading Comprehension:** Ask students questions about the introduction.

   What kind of document is the Constitution of the United States?
   When did the Constitution establish our system of government?
   Do we have the same system of government today?
   What is the introduction to the Constitution called?
   What are the three famous words that the Preamble begins with?
   What do these words describe?
   Who gives power to the government?
   Who serves the people?

3. **Listening:** With books closed, have students listen to the introduction and the excerpt in the box—presented by you or on the audio program.

4. **Reading:** Have students read along silently as they listen to the passage again—presented by you or on the audio program.

5. **Choral Reading:** Have students read the passage aloud in unison, along with you or the audio program.

6. Ask students if they understand the general meaning of the passage. (They do not have to know the exact meaning of unfamiliar words.)

7. **Public Speaking Practice:** Have individual students present the excerpted passage to the class. If you feel it is appropriate to do so, help students with their diction and projection to improve their public speaking skills in English.

8. **Pair Practice:** Have students work in pairs, taking turns reading the passage to each other. Circulate around the room and check students' reading and pronunciation, focusing more attention on students who need more assistance.

EXPANSION

Have an oratorical contest. Have interested students memorize the Preamble and present it to the class. Have class members vote on the best rendition, and award a prize to the winner.

TEXT PAGE 144: DOCUMENT OF FREEDOM: *The Bill of Rights*

FOCUS

> #### TOPIC
> The Bill of Rights
>
> #### GRAMMAR
>
> **Present Tense: Review**
>
> Changes in the Constitution **are** called amendments.
> The Bill of Rights give**s** rights and freedoms to all people in the U.S.
> They **have** the right to go to court.
>
> **Past Tense: Was/Were**
>
> These ten amendments **were** added to the Constitution in 1791.

NEW VOCABULARY

accuse	person
add	police
crime	protect
fair	quick
lawyer	trial
non-citizen	

PREVIEWING THE STORY

Have students talk about the story title and the illustration to establish the context of the story. Ask some or all of the following questions:

   What are rights?
   What is this document?
   Who is it for?
   What freedoms and rights do you have because you live in the United States?

READING THE STORY

1. Have students read the story silently.

2. **Check Reading Comprehension:** Ask students a question about each line of the story. For beginning-level students, ask these questions in the order below, so that the questions follow the sequence of the story. For higher-level students, ask the questions in random order.

   Can the people of the United States change the Constitution?
   What are changes in the Constitution called?
   How many amendments are there?

   What are the first ten amendments called?
   When were these amendments added to the Constitution?
   Who does the Bill of Rights give rights and freedoms to?
   Whose rights are guaranteed by the Constitution and the Bill of Rights?

   Which amendment guarantees freedom of speech?
   Which amendment guarantees freedom of the press?
   Which amendment guarantees freedom of religion?

   Which amendment guarantees freedom of assembly?
   Does the Bill of Rights guarantee the rights of people accused of crimes?
   What rights do people accused of crimes have?
   Where else does the Bill of Rights protect people?
   What do police need before they can go into a person's home?

3. Ask students if they have any questions about the story; check understanding of vocabulary.

4. **Class Circle Reading:** Have students read the story aloud as a class, with different students reading each line. (You can assign each line to a particular student or by seating patterns, or by letting students take turns spontaneously. In large classes, have a different group or row of students read each line.)

5. **Pair Practice:** Have students work in pairs, reading the passage to each other paragraph by paragraph. Circulate around the room and check students' reading and pronunciation, focusing more attention on students who need more assistance.

TEXT PAGE 145: *Check-Up*

MATCHING

> 1. c
> 2. d
> 3. b
> 4. a

> 7. Freedom of speech, the press, religion, assembly. The right to go to court, have a lawyer, have a fair and quick trial. The right not to allow police into your home without a document from the courts.

DID YOU UNDERSTAND?

Have students answer questions 1–6 in full sentences. Students can use short answers for question 7.

> 1. Yes, they can.
> 2. They are called amendments.
> 3. There are 27 amendments to the Constitution.
> 4. They are called the Bill of Rights.
> 5. The rights of citizens and non-citizens are guaranteed.
> 6. The first amendment guarantees freedom of speech.

DISCUSSION

Have students discuss these topics first in pairs or small groups, and then as a class.

1. Have students discuss the importance of the Bill of Rights in their everyday lives. What can they do in the United States because of the freedoms guaranteed by the Bill of Rights?

2. Have students discuss examples from current events of particular rights and freedoms that are not allowed elsewhere in the world.

TEXT PAGE 146: INTERVIEW:
Let's See What You Know About the Constitution

FOCUS

TOPICS

The Constitution
The Bill of Rights

GRAMMAR

Present Tense: Review

Do you know what the Constitution is?
I'm afraid I **don't** remember.

Past Tense: Regular Verbs

I studi**ed** that in my class.

Past Tense: Was/Were

That **was** a difficult question.

FUNCTIONAL INTERVIEW SKILLS

Reporting Information
Handling Not Knowing an Answer
Indicating Understanding
Hesitating

NEW VOCABULARY

difficult
That's okay.

PRACTICING THE DIALOG

1. **Setting the Scene:** Have students look at the photograph and determine who is talking: an INS examiner and an applicant. Establish the context: "The INS examiner is asking questions about the Constitution."

2. **Listening:** With books still closed, have students listen to the dialog—presented by you, by a pair of students, or on the audio program.

3. **Choral Repetition:** With books still closed, model each line and have the whole class repeat in unison.

4. **Reading:** With books open, have students follow along as two students present the dialog. Ask students if they have any questions and check understanding of vocabulary.

5. **Choral Conversation Practice:** Divide the class in half. Have Group 1 ask the questions and Group 2 give the answers; then reverse. (Or: You ask the questions and have the whole class answer in unison; then reverse.)

6. Call on one or two pairs of students to present the model dialog.

7. **Pair Practice:** Have students practice the dialog in pairs, taking turns being the INS examiner and the applicant.

8. Call on one or two more pairs of students to present the dialog to the class.

Dialog Notes

Line 6: The applicant repeats a fragment of the examiner's question ("The introduction to the Constitution?") and then says "Hmm." This illustrates the important functional interview strategy of Hesitating. The applicant is thinking of how to answer the examiner's question. By filling this thinking time with these expressions, he is letting the examiner know that he has heard the question and is trying to formulate an answer. Very often, students do not fill this thinking time with any language, which therefore leaves the questioner uncertain whether she has been heard or understood.

Line 6: ("I studied that in my class, but I don't remember the word.") Since the applicant cannot answer the question, he states that he has studied the subject matter in school but cannot remember the particular word the examiner is asking for. By doing this, the applicant is conveying in English the fact that he is making an effort to study civics in a class and that his inability to answer this particular question does not mean he has not learned other civics information.

Line 11: Encourage students to give at least three pieces of information when they are asked a very general open-ended question, such as "Tell me about some of the rights guaranteed by the Bill of Rights."

A. Now let's see what you know about the United States Constitution.
B. All right.
A. Do you know what the Constitution is?
B. Yes. It's *the supreme law of the land.*
A. And what is the introduction to the Constitution called?
B. The introduction to the Constitution? Hmm. I'm afraid I don't remember. I studied that in my class, but I don't remember the word.
A. That's okay. That WAS a difficult question. It's called the Preamble.

B. Oh, yes. The Preamble.
A. Do you know what the first ten amendments to the Constitution are called?
B. *The Bill of Rights.*
A. That's correct. Tell me about some of the rights guaranteed by the Bill of Rights.
B. Let me see. *Freedom of speech, freedom of the press, freedom of religion, and freedom of assembly.*

TEXT PAGE 147: PRESIDENTIAL PROFILE: *George Washington*

FOCUS

TOPIC

George Washington

GRAMMAR

Past Tense: Was/Were

George Washington **was** the leader of the Colonial Army.

Past Tense: Regular and Irregular Verbs

The American people respect**ed** him very much. He serv**ed** two terms.

At this meeting the representatives **wrote** the Constitution.
In 1789 George Washington **became** the first President of the United States.

NEW VOCABULARY

respect

GETTING READY

Have students identify George Washington as the person on the quarter and on the dollar bill.

PREVIEWING THE STORY

Have students talk about the story title and the photograph to establish the context of the story. Ask some or all of the following questions:

Who is this man?
What do you know about him?
What places in the United States are named after George Washington?

READING THE STORY

1. Have students read the story silently.
2. **Check Reading Comprehension:** Ask students a question about each line of the story. For beginning-level students, ask these questions in the order below, so that the questions follow the sequence of the story. For higher-level students, ask the questions in random order.

Who was the leader of the Colonial Army during the Revolutionary War?
Was he a good leader?
How did the American people feel about him?

What was George Washington the leader of in 1787?
What happened at that meeting?

When did George Washington become the first President of the United States?
How many terms did he serve?

Was George Washington an important person in American history?
What do Americans call him?

3. Ask students if they have any questions about the story; check understanding of vocabulary.

4. **Class Circle Reading:** Have students read the story aloud as a class, with different students reading each line. (You can assign each line to a particular student or by seating patterns, or by letting students take turns spontaneously. In large classes, have a different group or row of students read each line.)

5. **Pair Practice:** Have students work in pairs, reading the passage to each other paragraph by paragraph. Circulate around the room and check students' reading and pronunciation, focusing more attention on students who need more assistance.

EXPANSION

1. Bring in a picture book about Washington, D.C. Share it with students, pointing out the Washington Monument, the Jefferson Memorial, the U.S. Capitol, and the Supreme Court building. Discuss with students what they can see if they visit the nation's capital.

2. Have students prepare short oral or written reports on George Washington. Ask them to include the following information:

   When was he born?
   Where was he born?
   Where did he live?
   What did he do?
   When was he President?
   When did he die?

TEXT PAGE 148: *Check-Up*

THE ANSWER IS "GEORGE WASHINGTON!"

1. George Washington.
2. George Washington.
3. George Washington.
4. George Washington.

LISTENING

In order to do the listening exercises, students will need to write the name of the first president on Line A and the current president on Line B. Have students complete the exercises as you play the audio program or read the following:

Answers

1. B	5. B
2. A	6. A
3. A	7. B
4. B	8. A

Listen carefully and circle A or B.

1. Who is the president of the United States?
2. Who was the first president of the United States?
3. Who was the commander-in-chief of the armed forces?
4. Who is the commander-in-chief of the armed forces?
5. Who works in the executive branch of the government?
6. Who worked in the executive branch of the government?
7. Who's the chief executive?
8. Who was the chief executive?

"MIRROR" QUESTIONS

Point out to students that the questions in the box are two different ways of asking about the same information. Have students practice both questions and answers, chorally and individually.

After students have written the answers to these questions on a separate sheet of paper, have them work in pairs, asking and answering the questions. Students can provide short answers to these questions.

1. The Constitution.
2. The supreme law of the land.

3. The legislative branch.
4. It makes the laws.

5. The judicial branch.
6. It explains the laws.

7. The executive branch.
8. It enforces the laws.

9. The Senate and the House of Representatives.
10. The two parts of Congress.

11. Amendments.
12. Changes in the Constitution of the United States.

13. The Bill of Rights.
14. The first ten amendments to the Constitution.

REVIEWING GOVERNMENT OFFICIALS

Have students work in pairs, taking turns asking and answering the questions. (For additional practice, students can write the answers to these questions on a separate sheet of paper.)

You can use this test as a standardized form of assessment to measure student achievement of the curriculum objectives in Chapter 8. The test consists of 20 multiple-choice items and five sentences for dictation.

To score the test on a scale of 100:

- For each correct multiple-choice item, score four points.

- For each dictation sentence, do a general evaluation of the correctness of words, spelling, punctuation, and legibility. Score each sentence as follows:

  4 (Excellent), **3** (Good), **2** (Fair), **1** (Poor), **0** (Unsatisfactory)

Students can write their answers in the text or on the reproducible Chapter Test Answer Sheet provided in the Appendix.

A. COMPLETE THE SENTENCES

1. C
2. A
3. D
4. B
5. D
6. B
7. D
8. A
9. C
10. C
11. B
12. A

B. ANSWER THE QUESTIONS

13. A
14. B
15. C
16. B
17. D
18. C
19. A
20. D

C. DICTATION

Have students write these sentences as you read each sentence twice or play the audio program:

1. The Constitution is the highest law in the land.

2. The Constitution gives many powers to the Congress.

3. George Washington was the first president of the United States.

4. Americans vote for the president in November.

5. Congress has the power to declare war.

PERFORMANCE-BASED ASSESSMENT

These civics enrichment activities are designed to promote students' active participation in class and in the civic life of the community—through projects, issues discussions, community tasks, field trips, and Internet activities. Reproducible performance-based assessment forms for use in evaluating and documenting student participation in these activities are included in the Appendix.

CIVIC PARTICIPATION

Review with students the rights guaranteed by the 1st Amendment, and have students discuss how people in your community exercise these rights. Have them brainstorm as a class examples of freedom of speech, freedom of the press, freedom of religion, and freedom of assembly. This discussion serves as preparation for the project activity that follows.

PROJECT ACTIVITY

1st Amendment Bulletin Board Project: In this project, students create a bulletin board display about rights guaranteed by the 1st Amendment. They cut out newspaper headlines and photographs that are examples of these rights and display them on the bulletin board. They should also write brief paragraphs about the different rights and the examples they find. Have students take responsibility for all aspects of this project. Have them identify the particular tasks involved in the project, who will accomplish each task, what resources are needed, and what form the final bulletin board display will take. Use the project as a basis for building students' skills in leadership, teamwork, and communicating information—key SCANS* skills useful for success in the workplace.

*Secretary's Commission on Achieving Necessary Skills

COMMUNITY ISSUES

Problem-Posing Discussion: Have students discuss limits on the rights guaranteed by the 1st Amendment. Point out the examples given in the text: a person can't shout "Fire!" in a movie theater; in some cities young people can't get together in large groups in public places. Have students give examples of limits on the rights guaranteed by the 1st Amendment, and have them share their opinions about these limits.

TECHNOLOGY ENRICHMENT

See Appendix page 160 for additional Internet enrichment activities related to this chapter.

<table>
<tr><td>

CHAPTER 9

</td><td>

OVERVIEW
Student Text
Pages 153–170

</td></tr>
</table>

TOPICS

The National Anthem
Expansion
The Civil War
Abraham Lincoln
Amendments

GRAMMAR

Past Tense
Ordinal Numbers

FUNCTIONAL INTERVIEW SKILLS

Reporting Information
Comprehending Rephrased Questions
Asking for Repetition
Hesitating

KEY VOCABULARY

PEOPLE	EVENTS	PLACES, COUNTRIES, GEOGRAPHY	
Abraham Lincoln	battle	Alaska	Mississippi River
African	Civil War	Arlington, Virginia	North
American	dedication	Baltimore Harbor	Northern states
Blacks	Emancipation	border	Oregon
British	Proclamation	California	Pacific Ocean
citizens	Gettysburg	Capitol Building	Pentagon
firefighter	Address	England	region
Francis Scott Key	national holiday	France	Russia
George Washington	Presidents' Day	Gettysburg National	South
leader	Revolutionary	Cemetery	Southern states
president	War	Gettysburg, Pennsylvania	Spain
slave	terrorist attack	Hawaii	Texas
speaker	war	Louisiana	United States
women	War of 1812	Mexico	western

VERBS

assassinate	fight	sell
attack	force	sign
become	free	speak
begin	give	stay together
burn	grow	transport
buy	help	use
celebrate	honor	vote
come	leave	want
disagree	make	watch
display	need	win
end	receive	work
establish	save	write
expand		

OTHER WORDS

address	history	slavery
cause	home	song
Confederacy	income taxes	speech
document	land	Star-Spangled
economics	minimum	Banner
factory	nation	state
famous	national	system
farm	anthem	taxes
farm products	overseas	territory
flag	plantation	treaty
fort	property	Union
freedoms	rights	voting age

RELATED PRACTICE

Foundations: Chapter 12
Word by Word Basic: pages 128–137
Word by Word: pages 75–78
Side by Side Book 2: Chapters 1–3
Side by Side Interactive CD-ROM / Side by Side TV Video: Level 2A, Segments 27–32
ExpressWays Book 1: Chapter 7

TEXT PAGE 153: *Vocabulary Preview*

You may want to introduce these words before beginning the chapter, or you may choose to wait until they first occur in a specific lesson. If you choose to introduce them at this point, here are some suggestions:

1. Have students look at the photographs on text page 153 and identify the words they already know.

2. Present the vocabulary. Say each word and have the class repeat it chorally and individually. Check students' understanding and pronunciation of the words.

3. Practice the vocabulary as a class, in pairs, or in small groups. Have students cover the word list and look at the photographs. Practice the words in the following ways:

   • Say a phrase and have students tell the number of the photograph.
   • Give the number of a photograph and have students say the phrase.

FOCUS

TOPIC

The National Anthem

GRAMMAR

Past Tense

Francis Scott Key **wrote** the *Star-Spangled Banner*.

The United States and England **fought** against each other in the War of 1812.

During the war the British burn**ed** the White House.

He watch**ed** the American flag at the fort.

NEW VOCABULARY

anthem	morning
attack	sing
Baltimore Harbor	song
battle	*Star-Spangled Banner*
British	then
burn	War of 1812
fort	watch

PREVIEWING THE STORY

Have students talk about the story title and the illustration to establish the context of the story. Ask some or all of the following questions:

> What's happening in this picture?
> Where are they?
> What are they looking at?
> What is an anthem?

READING THE STORY

1. Have students read the story silently.

2. **Check Reading Comprehension:** Ask students a question about each line of the story. For beginning-level students, ask these questions in the order below so that the questions follow the sequence of the story. For higher-level students, ask the questions in random order.

   > What is the name of the national anthem of the United States?
   > Who wrote the *Star-Spangled Banner*?
   > What's the song about?
   >
   > Who fought in the War of 1812?
   > What did the British burn during the war?
   > What did they attack in Baltimore Harbor?
   > Who watched the battle?
   > What did he watch at the fort?
   > What happened the next morning?
   > Who won the battle?
   > What did Key do?

3. Ask students if they have any questions about the story; check understanding of vocabulary.

4. **Choral Repetition:** Read aloud each line of the story and have students repeat.

5. **Class Circle Reading:** Have students read the story aloud as a class, with different students reading each line. (You can assign each line to a particular student or by seating patterns, or by letting students take turns spontaneously. In large classes, have a different group or row of students read each line.)

6. **Pair Practice:** Have students work in pairs, reading the passage to each other paragraph by paragraph. Circulate around the room and check students' reading and pronunciation, focusing more attention on students who need more assistance.

TEXT PAGE 155: SONG OF FREEDOM:
The Star-Spangled Banner (The National Anthem)

PRACTICING THE SONG

1. **Listening to the Lyrics:** Have students listen to the lyrics of the song by playing the audio or saying the lyrics yourself.

2. **Choral Repetition:** Read aloud each line of the song and have students repeat in unison.

3. **Listening to the Song:** Have students listen to the song by playing the audio or singing it yourself.

4. **Singing Aloud:** Play the instrumental version of the song and have students sing along. (The instrumental version follows the vocal version on the audio program.)

YOUR NATIVE COUNTRY'S NATIONAL ANTHEM

Have students discuss their native countries' national anthems and then sing them for the class.

EXPANSION

Discuss with students the photo (and caption) of the flag being displayed by firefighters standing on the roof of the Pentagon after the terrorist attack on September 11, 2001.

TEXT PAGE 156: *Expansion*

FOCUS

> ### TOPIC
> Expansion
>
> ### GRAMMAR
>
> **Past Tense**
>
> In the 1800s the United States expand**ed** to the Pacific Ocean.
> Americans want**ed** more land for homes and farms.
>
> It **bought** Florida from Spain.
> Russia **sold** Alaska to the United States.
> Hawaii **became** a territory.
>
> **Ordinal Numbers**
>
> Alaska and Hawaii are the **49th** and **50th** states of the Union.

NEW VOCABULARY

after	Louisiana	sell
Alaska	Mississippi	territory
buy	River	transport
expand	Oregon	treaty
farm	product	Union
Florida	region	use
Hawaii	Russia	western border

PREVIEWING THE STORY

Have students talk about the story title and the map to establish the context of the story. Ask some or all of the following questions:

> What is this a map of?
> What do the dates mean?
> Where is our state located?
> What was the western border of the United States in 1783? in 1803? in 1845?

READING THE STORY

1. Have students read the story silently.

2. **Check Reading Comprehension:** Ask students a question about each line of the story. For beginning-level students, ask these questions in the order below so that the questions follow the sequence of the story. For higher-level students, ask the questions in random order.

> Where did the United States expand to in the 1800s?
> Why did Americans want more land?
> What did they want to use the Mississippi River for?
> Where was the western border of the United States after the Revolutionary War?
> How did the United States expand to the Louisiana region?
> How did the United States expand into Florida?
> When did California and Texas become part of the United States?
> How did the United States expand to the Oregon country?
> How did Alaska become part of the United States?
> What area became a territory of the United States?
> What are the 49th and 50th states of the Union?

3. Ask students if they have any questions about the story; check understanding of vocabulary.

4. **Choral Repetition:** Read aloud each line of the story and have students repeat.

5. **Class Circle Reading:** Have students read the story aloud as a class, with different students reading each line. (You can assign each line to a particular student or by seating patterns, or by letting students take turns spontaneously. In large classes, have a different group or row of students read each line.)

6. **Pair Practice:** Have students work in pairs, reading the passage to each other paragraph by paragraph. Circulate around the room and check students' reading and pronunciation, focusing more attention on students who need more assistance.

EXPANSION

1. Bring in a current map of the United States. Have students identify in which territories current states are located. (For example, Washington in the Oregon country; California in the Mexican Cession.)

2. If you have students from Mexico in your class, have them discuss the Texas Annexation and the Mexican Cession. Ask them what they learned about this when they studied history in school in their native country. How did their country react at that time? How do people in their country feel today about what happened? How would the United States be different today if this had not happened?

TEXT PAGE 157: *Check-Up*

DID YOU UNDERSTAND?

1. Louisiana
2. Florida
3. California
4. Alaska
5. Oregon

YOUR STATE

Have students answer with the appropriate information.

ANSWER THESE QUESTIONS

1. Americans wanted more land for homes and farms.
2. Texas and California.
3. Alaska and Hawaii.

TEXT PAGES 158–159: *The Civil War*

FOCUS

TOPIC

The Civil War

GRAMMAR

Past Tense

The North and the South **fought** the Civil War from 1861 to 1865.
The Southern states **said** they needed slaves to work on the farms.

One main cause of the Civil War **was** slavery.
The Northern states **were** also called the Union.

NEW VOCABULARY

African	expensive	plantation
cause	factory	property
Civil War	force	slavery
confederacy	leave	Union
disagree	overseas	
economics	owner	

PREVIEWING THE STORY

(This reading passage has four sections, each introduced by a photograph. You may want to treat each section as a separate story, previewing and reading one section before going on to the next.)

Have students talk about the story title and the photographs to establish the context of the story. Ask some or all of the following questions:

Page 158 (top):

What's happening in this picture?
Who are these people?
How many people do you think there are?
How do the people in this picture feel?
What is a civil war?

Page 158 (bottom):

Who are these people?
What are they doing?
Where are they from?
Where are they in this picture?
What are they thinking?/How do they feel?

Page 159 (top):

(Point to the picture on the left.)
What do you see in the picture? (A factory.)
Do you think this is in the North or the South? (North.)
What kind of jobs do people have in this place?
What kind of life do people have there?

(Point to the picture on the right.)
What do you see in the picture? (A plantation.)
Do you think this is in the North or the South? (South.)
What kind of jobs do people have in this place?
What kind of life do people have there?

Page 159 (bottom):

Who is this man?
What did he do?
Where have you seen his face before?

READING THE STORY

1. Have students read the story silently.
2. **Check Reading Comprehension:** Ask students a question about each line of the story. For beginning-level students, ask these questions in the order below so that the questions follow the sequence of the story. For higher-level students, ask the questions in random order.

    Who fought in the Civil War?
    When was the Civil War?
    What were the Northern states called?
    What were the Southern states called?

What was one main cause of the Civil War?
Who were slaves?
Did slaves have any rights or freedoms?
What did their owners do?
Why did the Southern states say they needed slaves?
What did the Northern states want to do?

What was another cause of the Civil War?
Who had many factories?
Who had many plantations?
What did the North and South disagree about?
What did these taxes do to the North and South?

Who was against slavery?
What happened after Lincoln became president?
When did the Civil War begin?
Who won the war?

3. Ask students if they have any questions about the story; check understanding of vocabulary.
4. **Choral Repetition:** Read aloud each line of the story and have students repeat.
5. **Class Circle Reading:** Have students read the story aloud as a class, with different students reading each line. (You can assign each line to a particular student or by seating patterns, or by letting students take turns spontaneously. In large classes, have a different group or row of students read each line.)
6. **Pair Practice:** Have students work in pairs, reading the passage to each other paragraph by paragraph. Circulate around the room and check students' reading and pronunciation, focusing more attention on students who need more assistance.

EXPANSION

1. Have students discuss civil wars in their native countries. What were the causes? the key people and events? the outcomes?
2. Have students discuss differences between how African-American people came to the United States and how people from other countries came as immigrants. Ask them what it would have been like to live as a slave before the Civil War.

FOCUS

TOPICS

Abraham Lincoln
The Civil War

GRAMMAR

Past Tense

Lincoln want**ed** to save the Union.
This document free**d** the slaves.

The North **won** the Civil War.
He **was** president during the Civil War.

Ordinal Numbers

Abraham Lincoln was the **sixteenth**
president of the United States.

NEW VOCABULARY

assassinate	Presidents' Day
Emancipation	save
Proclamation	sixteenth
free (v.)	together
great	
honor	

GETTING READY

Have students identify the person whose face is on
the penny and the five dollar bill.

PREVIEWING THE STORY

Have students talk about the story title and the
photograph to establish the context of the story. Ask
some or all of the following questions:

What is this? (A statue/monument.)
Who is he?
Where is this?
Why do we have this memorial?

READING THE STORY

1. Have students read the story silently.

2. **Check Reading Comprehension:** Ask
   students a question about each line of the story.
   For beginning-level students, ask these questions
   in the order below so that the questions follow
   the sequence of the story. For higher-level
   students, ask the questions in random order.

   Who was the sixteenth president of the
      United States?
   Who was president of the United States
      during the Civil War?
   Who was the leader of the Northern states
      during the Civil War?
   What did he want to save?
   What did he want the Northern and Southern
      states to do?

   How did Lincoln feel about slavery?
   What did he sign in 1863?
   What did the Emancipation Proclamation do?

   Which side won the Civil War? When?
   What happened to President Lincoln five days
      after the war ended?

   What kind of president was Abraham Lincoln?
   When do Americans celebrate Presidents' Day?
   Who do Americans honor on Presidents' Day?

3. Ask students if they have any questions about
   the story; check understanding of vocabulary.

4. **Choral Repetition:** Read aloud each line of the
   story and have students repeat.

5. **Class Circle Reading:** Have students read the
   story aloud as a class, with different students
   reading each line. (You can assign each line to a
   particular student or by seating patterns, or by
   letting students take turns spontaneously. In
   large classes, have a different group or row of
   students read each line.)

6. **Pair Practice:** Have students work in pairs,
   reading the passage to each other paragraph by
   paragraph. Circulate around the room and check
   students' reading and pronunciation, focusing
   more attention on students who need more
   assistance.

EXPANSION

Bring in a picture book about Washington, D.C.
Point out the Lincoln Memorial and Ford's Theatre
(site of Lincoln's assassination.)

TEXT PAGE 161: *Check-Up*

VOCABULARY CHECK

1. Confederacy
2. slavery
3. plantations
4. rights
5. Union

THE ANSWER IS "ABRAHAM LINCOLN!"

1. Abraham Lincoln.
2. Abraham Lincoln.
3. Abraham Lincoln.
4. Abraham Lincoln.

DID YOU UNDERSTAND?

Have students answer these questions using full sentences.

1. The Civil War was a war between the states in the North and the states in the South.
2. Two causes of the war were slavery and economics.

TEXT PAGE 162: VOICE OF FREEDOM: *Lincoln's Gettysburg Address*

(As noted in the text, this lesson is provided for enrichment and speaking practice. It is not required for the INS interview.)

FOCUS

TOPIC

Abraham Lincoln

GRAMMAR

Past Tense

Abraham Lincoln **was** an excellent speaker. He **gave** his most famous speech in Gettysburg, Pennsylvania.

NEW VOCABULARY

cemetery	soldier
dedication	speaker
Gettysburg	speech
nation	voice

GETTING READY

Bring in a map of the United States and have students locate Pennsylvania and Gettysburg.

PREVIEWING THE STORY

Have students talk about the story title and the illustration to establish the context of the story. Ask some or all of the following questions:

Who is this man?
What's he doing?
Where's Gettysburg?
What's an *address*?

READING THE STORY

1. Have students first read the introductory sentences silently.

2. **Check Reading Comprehension:** Ask students questions about the introduction.

   Was Abraham Lincoln a good speaker?
   Where did he give his most famous speech? When?
   What event did he speak at?
   What happened there four months before his speech?
   What is Lincoln's speech called?

3. **Listening:** With books closed, have students listen to the introduction and the excerpt in the box—presented by you or on the audio program.

4. **Reading:** Have students read along silently as they listen to the passage again—presented by you or on the audio program.

5. **Choral Reading:** Have students read the passage aloud in unison, along with you or the audio program.

6. Ask students if they understand the general meaning of the passage. (They do not have to know the exact meaning of unfamiliar words.)

7. **Public Speaking Practice:** Have individual students present the excerpted passage to the class. If you feel it is appropriate to do so, help students with their diction and projection to improve their public speaking skills in English.

8. **Pair Practice:** Have students work in pairs, taking turns reading the passage to each other. Circulate around the room and check students' reading and pronunciation, focusing more attention on students who need more assistance.

EXPANSION

1. Have an oratorical contest. Have interested students memorize the excerpt of Lincoln's Gettysburg Address and present it to the class. Have class members vote on the best rendition, and award a prize to the winner.

2. Bring in a picture book about the Battle of Gettysburg. Share it with the students, and discuss with them how great the loss of life was during that battle. Mention to students that much of the battlefield area is preserved and is a major tourist attraction in Pennsylvania.

TEXT PAGES 163: INTERVIEW:
What's the National Anthem of the United States?

FOCUS

TOPICS

The *Star-Spangled Banner*
The Civil War
Abraham Lincoln

GRAMMAR

Past Tense

What **did** the Emancipation Proclamation do?
Abraham Lincoln sign**ed** the Emancipation Proclamation.
Do you know who **wrote** it?

FUNCTIONAL INTERVIEW SKILLS

Reporting Information
Comprehending Rephrased Questions
Asking for Repetition
Hesitating

NEW VOCABULARY

---
minute

PRACTICING THE DIALOG

1. **Setting the Scene:** Have students look at the photo and determine who is talking: an INS

examiner and an applicant. Establish the context: "The INS examiner is asking questions about the national anthem, the Civil War, and Abraham Lincoln."

2. **Listening:** With books closed, have students listen to the dialog—presented by you, by a pair of students, or on the audio program.

3. **Choral Repetition:** With books still closed, model each line and have the whole class repeat in unison.

4. **Reading:** With books open, have students follow along as two students present the dialog. Ask students if they have any questions and check understanding of vocabulary.

5. **Choral Conversation Practice:** Divide the class in half. Have Group 1 ask the questions and Group 2 give the answers; then reverse. (Or: You ask the questions and have the whole class answer in unison; then reverse.)

6. Call on one or two pairs of students to present the dialog.

7. **Pair Practice:** Have students practice the dialog in pairs, taking turns being the INS examiner and the applicant.

8. Call on one or two more pairs of students to present the dialog to the class.

Dialog Notes

Line 4: The applicant uses the expression "Hmm. Let me think for a minute" to fill time while she prepares to answer the question.

Line 8: The applicant politely asks the examiner to repeat the question.

Line 9: Trying to be helpful to the applicant, the examiner reformulates the question and gives the additional information that the Emancipation Proclamation has something to do with Abraham Lincoln and the Civil War. This may indeed sometimes help, but at other times it may lead to more confusion. Students should know that if the question seems even more difficult the second time it is asked, it may be that the examiner is trying to help by using different words or adding some more information.

A. What's the national anthem of the United States?
B. *The Star-Spangled Banner.*
A. That's right. Do you know who wrote it?
B. Hmm. Let me think for a minute. I think it was *Francis Scott Key.*
A. That's correct. Can you tell me who the president was during the Civil War?
B. *Abraham Lincoln.*
A. And what did the Emancipation Proclamation do?
B. I'm sorry. Could you please repeat that?
A. Yes. Abraham Lincoln signed the Emancipation Proclamation during the Civil War. Do you know what it did?
B. Hmm. Oh, yes. It *freed the slaves.*
A. Very good.

TEXT PAGE 164: *Amendments to the Constitution*

FOCUS

> ### TOPIC
> Amendments
>
> ### GRAMMAR
>
> **Past Tense**
>
> The 13th Amendment end**ed** slavery.
>
> The 14th Amendment **made** all Blacks citizens of the United States.
> The 19th Amendment **gave** women the right to vote.
>
> **Ordinal Numbers**
>
> The **13th** Amendment ended slavery.
> The **15th** Amendment gave Blacks the right to vote.
> The **26th** Amendment gave citizens 18 years old and older the right to vote.

NEW VOCABULARY

> Blacks
> minimum
> soon

PREVIEWING THE STORY

Have students talk about the story title and the photographs to establish the context of the story. Ask some or all of the following questions:

> What is the Constitution?
> What is an amendment?
>
> (Point to the photo on the left.)
> What are these people doing?
> Where are they?
> What does the sign on the wall say?
>
> (Point to the photo on the right.)
> Who are these people?
> Where are they?
> When do you think this photograph was taken?
> What do they want?

READING THE STORY

1. Have students read the story silently.
2. **Check Reading Comprehension:** Ask students a question about each line of the story. For beginning-level students, ask these questions in the order below so that the questions follow the sequence of the story. For higher-level students, ask the questions in random order.

> What are changes in the Constitution called?
> How many amendments are there?
> What is the Bill of Rights?
> Are the other amendments important?

After what war were there three important
amendments?

What did the 13th Amendment do?

Which amendment made all Blacks citizens of
the United States?

What did the 15th Amendment do?

Which amendment established income taxes?

When did women get the right to vote?

What did the 26th Amendment do?

What is the minimum voting age in the United
States?

3. Ask students if they have any questions about
the story; check understanding of vocabulary.

4. **Choral Repetition:** Read aloud each line of the
story and have the students repeat.

5. **Class Circle Reading:** Have students read the
story aloud as a class, with different students
reading each line. (You can assign each line to a
particular student or by seating patterns, or by
letting students take turns spontaneously. In
large classes, have a different group or row of
students read each line.)

6. **Pair Practice:** Have students work in pairs,
reading the passage to each other paragraph by
paragraph. Circulate around the room and check
students' reading and pronunciation, focusing
more attention on students who need more
assistance.

TEXT PAGE 165: *Check-Up*

ORDINAL NUMBERS

1. 16th (sixteenth)
2. 1st (first)
3. 49th (forty-ninth)
4. 50th (fiftieth)
5. 18th (eighteenth)
6. 19th (nineteenth)

MATCHING

16th - established income taxes
19th - gave women the right to vote
13th - ended slavery
26th - gave citizens 18 and older the right to vote
15th - gave Blacks the right to vote

TEXT PAGE 166: *Check-Up*

VOCABULARY CHECK

1. slavery
2. women
3. income
4. age
5. right

QUESTIONS AND ANSWERS

This exercise offers students important practice with
the multiple ways a question might be posed by the
INS examiner. First, have students repeat each
question after you. Then, have students practice
asking and answering the questions with other
students. Finally, have students write their answers
to the questions.

LISTENING

In order to do the listening exercises, students will need to write the name of the current president of the United States on line D. Have students complete the exercises as you play the audio program or read the following:

Listen carefully and circle A, B, C, or D.

1. Who was the first president of the United States?
2. Who was the president during the Civil War?
3. Who wrote the Declaration of Independence?
4. Who's the president of the United States?
5. Who was the third president of the United States?
6. Who is called "the father of our country"?

Answers

1. A	4. D
2. C	5. B
3. B	6. A

TEXT PAGE 167: *Review*

TALKING TIME LINE: *Important Dates in U.S. History*

Have students complete the time line. Then have them work in pairs, asking and answering the questions at the bottom of the page, based on the information recorded on the time line.

1787	Representatives wrote the Constitution.
1791	The Bill of Rights was added to the Constitution.
1861	The Civil War began.
1863	President Lincoln signed the Emancipation Proclamation.
1865	The Civil War ended.
1920	Women got the right to vote.

You can use this test as a standardized form of assessment to measure student achievement of the curriculum objectives in Chapter 9. The test consists of 20 multiple-choice items and five sentences for dictation.

To score the test on a scale of 100:

- For each correct multiple-choice item, score four points.

- For each dictation sentence, do a general evaluation of the correctness of words, spelling, punctuation, and legibility. Score each sentence as follows:

    4 (Excellent), **3** (Good), **2** (Fair), **1** (Poor), **0** (Unsatisfactory)

Students can write their answers in the text or on the reproducible Chapter Test Answer Sheet provided in the Appendix.

A. COMPLETE THE SENTENCES

1. C
2. D
3. A
4. C
5. B
6. C
7. A
8. D
9. C
10. B
11. C
12. D

B. ANSWER THE QUESTIONS

13. A
14. D
15. D
16. B
17. A
18. B
19. C
20. B

C. DICTATION

Have students write these sentences as you read each sentence twice or play the audio program:

1. America's national song is about the flag.
2. The Constitution of the United States has twenty-seven (27) amendments.
3. Abraham Lincoln was the president during the Civil War.
4. The Civil War was a war between the North and the South.
5. Presidents' Day is a national holiday in February.

PERFORMANCE-BASED ASSESSMENT

These civics enrichment activities are designed to promote students' active participation in class and in the civic life of the community—through projects, issues discussions, community tasks, field trips, and Internet activities. Reproducible performance-based assessment forms for use in evaluating and documenting student participation in these activities are included in the Appendix.

CIVIC PARTICIPATION

Bring to class copies of the U.S. Constitution. In small groups, have students look at the Constitution and find the amendments that they studied in this chapter. Then have each group discuss ideas for a new amendment to the Constitution and write a proposed amendment. Groups should present their new amendments to the entire class and give reasons why they think their amendments are important.

DEBATE ACTIVITY

Have students participate in a classroom debate about the voting age in the United States. Divide the class into two teams, or have students choose their teams based on the position they want to take. Each team should take one of these positions:

a) The minimum voting age in the United States should be eighteen, as it is now.

b) The minimum voting age should be twenty-one.

INTERNET ACTIVITY

Have students go to the websites listed in the text for the Fort McHenry National Monument in Maryland, the Gettysburg National Military Park in Pennsylvania, and the National Park Service in Washington, D.C. Have them take the virtual tours, browse the websites for additional information about the locations, and write sentences about what they see and the information they find. Students can do this Internet activity individually, in pairs, or in small groups based on the computer resources available. Make sure students have the basic skills needed to access the Internet, such as using a computer keyboard and mouse and performing such tasks as clicking, scrolling, dragging, and typing URLs to access websites.

TECHNOLOGY ENRICHMENT

See Appendix page 160 for additional Internet enrichment activities related to this chapter.

<table>
<tr><td>

CHAPTER
10

</td><td>

OVERVIEW
Student Text
Pages 171–196

</td></tr>
</table>

TOPICS

Industrial Revolution
Labor Movement
Immigration
20th-Century History
Civil Rights Movement
Citizens' Rights & Responsibilities
Presidents: 1961–Present
September 11, 2001

GRAMMAR

Past Tense
Can
Should
Must

FUNCTIONAL INTERVIEW SKILLS

Reporting Information
Clarifying Ambiguous Questions

KEY VOCABULARY

PEOPLE

actor	Jimmy Carter
American	John F. Kennedy
Bill Clinton	leader
Black	Lyndon B. Johnson
candidate	Native American
citizen	official
factory worker	President
family	Reverend Martin
farmer	Luther King, Jr.
Franklin D.	Richard Nixon
Roosevelt	Ronald Reagan
George Bush	terrorist
George W. Bush	troops
Gerald Ford	Vice President
immigrant	victim
Japanese	worker

EVENTS/HISTORICAL PERIODS

civil rights movement	recession
Cold War	Vietnam War
Depression	war
election	Watergate
Election Day	World War I
Great Society	World War II
Gulf War	
impeachment trial	**INVENTIONS**
Industrial Revolution	cotton gin
Korean War	light bulb
Labor Day	machine
March on Washington	phonograph
national holiday	sewing machine
New Deal	telephone
Operation Desert Storm	typewriter

PLACES & COUNTRIES		VERBS		OTHER WORDS	
Afghanistan	Nagasaki	acquit	kill	administration	politics
Arlington,	New Jersey	assassinate	lead	airplane	protest
Virginia	New York	attack	lose	Allied Nations	railroad
Austria-Hungary	City	celebrate	obey	armed forces	Republican
Bosnia	Pearl Harbor	choose	pay	assassination	salary
Boston	Pennsylvania	collapse	produce	atomic bomb	scandal
China	Pentagon	compete	raise	civil rights	Social Security
East Coast	Russia	count	reduce	communist	system
England	Somalia	crash	reform	Democratic	social services
Florida	Soviet Union	die	regulate	demonstration	speech
France	United States	discuss	remember	discrimination	stock market
Germany	Vietnam	elect	resign	equal rights	taxes
Hawaii	Washington,	expand	shoot	expansion	terrorism
Hiroshima	D.C.	fight	spend	human rights	union
Italy	West Coast	hijack	stop	immigration	United Nations
Japan	World Trade	impeach	support	labor union	(UN)
Kosovo	Center	improve	take office	national debt	vote
Lincoln Memorial		invent	win	peace	welfare system
				police department	world power

RELATED PRACTICE

Foundations: Chapter 13
Word by Word Basic: pages 138–149
Word by Word: pages 80–85
Side by Side Book 2: Chapters 4, 5
Side by Side Interactive CD-ROM / Side by Side TV Video: Level 2A, Segments 33–36
ExpressWays Book 1: Chapter 8

TEXT PAGE 171: *Vocabulary Preview*

You may want to introduce these words before beginning the chapter, or you may choose to wait until they first occur in a specific lesson. If you choose to introduce them at this point, here are some suggestions:

1. Have students look at the photographs on text page 171 and identify the words they already know.

2. Present the vocabulary. Say each word and have the class repeat it chorally and individually. Check students' understanding and pronunciation of the words.

3. Practice the vocabulary as a class, in pairs, or in small groups. Have students cover the word list and look at the photographs. Practice the words in the following ways:

   • Say a word or phrase and have students tell the number of the photograph.
   • Give the number of a photograph and have students say the word or phrase.

FOCUS

TOPIC

Industrial Revolution

GRAMMAR

Past Tense

In the 1790s the first factories open**ed** in the United States.

The first Americans **were** farmers.
The railroads **went** across the country.

NEW VOCABULARY

across	industrial	phonograph
clothing	invent	produce
cotton gin	invention	railroad
fast	light bulb	sewing
grow	machine	machine
immigrant	open	typewriter

PREVIEWING THE STORY

Have students talk about the story title and the photographs to establish the context of the story. Ask some or all of the following questions:

What is the man in the first picture doing?
Why is everyone watching?
Who is he? (Alexander Graham Bell)

What is the woman in the second picture doing?
Where does she work?

READING THE STORY

1. Have students read the story silently.

2. **Check Reading Comprehension:** Ask students a question about each line of the story. For beginning-level students, ask these questions in the order below so that the questions follow the sequence of the story. For higher-level students, ask the questions in random order.

What work did the first Americans do?
When did the first American factories open?
What were two important inventions?
What did the United States do with these machines?

What else did Americans invent?
Where did the railroads go?

Where were the factories?/What happened to the cities?
Where did people come from to work in the factories?

3. Ask students if they have any questions about the story; check understanding of vocabulary.

4. **Choral Repetition:** Read aloud each line of the story and have students repeat.

5. **Class Circle Reading:** Have students read the story aloud as a class, with different students reading each line. (You can assign each line to a particular student or by seating patterns, or by letting students take turns spontaneously. In large classes, have a different group or row of students read each line.)

6. **Pair Practice:** Have students work in pairs, reading the passage to each other paragraph by paragraph. Circulate around the room and check students' reading and pronunciation, focusing more attention on students who need more assistance.

EXPANSION

1. Have students share information about whether their home town in their native country had farms or industry, or both. Have them discuss the importance of farming and/or industry in their native country. Have them describe their countries' most important farm and industry products.

2. Have students discuss what they think was the most important invention in history and explain the reasons for their answers.

TEXT PAGE 173: *The Labor Movement*

FOCUS

TOPIC

Labor Movement

GRAMMAR

Past Tense

They usually work**ed** twelve hours a day.
Factory workers **had** a difficult life.
Their pay **was** low.

NEW VOCABULARY

---

belong	low
get hurt	pay
group	safe
Labor Day	worker
labor movement	workplace
labor union	

PREVIEWING THE STORY

Have students talk about the story title and the photograph to establish the context of the story. Ask some or all of the following questions:

What are these women doing?
What does *picket* mean?
What is a striker?
What are tailors?
Have you ever seen people picketing?
Why do people picket/go on strike?
Do you know of any group that is on strike now?

READING THE STORY

1. Have students read the story silently.
2. **Check Reading Comprehension:** Ask students a question about each line of the story. For beginning-level students, ask these questions in the order below so that the questions follow the sequence of the story. For higher-level students, ask the questions in random order.

What kind of life did factory workers have?
How long did they usually work?
How was their pay?

Why did many workers get hurt?
What did they begin to do?
What were the workers' groups called?
What did the unions fight for?
Do people still belong to unions today?

When do Americans celebrate Labor Day?
What does this holiday celebrate?

3. Ask students if they have any questions about the story; check understanding of vocabulary.
4. **Choral Repetition:** Read aloud each line of the story and have students repeat.
5. **Class Circle Reading:** Have students read the story aloud as a class, with different students reading each line. (You can assign each line to a particular student or by seating patterns, or by letting students take turns spontaneously. In large classes, have a different group or row of students read each line.)
6. **Pair Practice:** Have students work in pairs, reading the passage to each other paragraph by paragraph. Circulate around the room and check students' reading and pronunciation, focusing more attention on students who need more assistance.

EXPANSION

1. Have students discuss a current strike or labor problem.
2. Have students discuss how Labor Day is celebrated in the United States, and how it is celebrated in their native countries.
3. Have students discuss what they can do if there are unsafe conditions at a workplace and the employer refuses to take care of them.

TEXT PAGES 174–175: *A Nation of Immigrants*

FOCUS

> ### TOPIC
> Immigration
>
> ### GRAMMAR
>
> **Past Tense**
>
> America needed farmers and workers.
> In the 1800s, America **grew** very quickly.

NEW VOCABULARY

allow	except	quickly
continue	farmland	stop
dangerous	limit	themselves

PREVIEWING THE STORY

Have students talk about the story title and the photographs to establish the context of the story. Ask some or all of the following questions:

Who are the people in the top picture?
Where are they from?
Where are they going? Why?
What is the man carrying?
What year do you think this picture was taken?

Who are the people in the middle picture?
Where are they from?
Where are they in this photograph?
What are they doing?
When do you think this picture was taken?

Who are the men in the bottom picture?
Where are they?
What are they looking for? Why?
Have you ever met a member of the border patrol?

READING THE STORY

1. Have students read the story silently.
2. **Check Reading Comprehension:** Ask students a question about each line of the story. For beginning-level students, ask these questions in the order below so that the questions follow the sequence of the story. For higher-level students, ask the questions in random order.

When did America grow quickly?
What did expansion and the industrial revolution do?
What did America need as it grew?
Who came from many countries?
Where did they work?
What did immigrants help build?

When did the U.S. begin to limit immigration?
What kind of laws did the government make?
When did a new immigration law change this?
What did the new law allow?

Do immigrants continue to come to the United States?
Why do immigrants come here?
Why is the United States called "a nation of immigrants?"

3. Ask students if they have any questions about the story; check understanding of vocabulary.

4. **Choral Repetition:** Read aloud each line of the story and have students repeat.

5. **Class Circle Reading:** Have students read the story aloud as a class, with different students reading each line. (You can assign each line to a particular student or by seating patterns, or by letting students take turns spontaneously. In large classes, have a different group or row of students read each line.)

6. **Pair Practice:** Have students work in pairs, reading the passage to each other paragraph by paragraph. Circulate around the room and check students' reading and pronunciation, focusing more attention on students who need more assistance.

EXPANSION

1. Have students imagine they are one of the people in the photographs on page 174. Have them describe what they are thinking and feeling.

2. **Immigrant Interviews:** Have students interview older immigrants who emigrated from different countries many years ago. (Senior citizen programs in many communities will gladly assist with this activity.) Have students report on the people they interviewed: when and why they came, where they settled, their life in the United States, etc.

VOCABULARY CHECK

1. sewing machine
2. labor unions
3. immigrants
4. laws
5. clothing

DISCUSSION

Have students discuss these questions in pairs or small groups and then share as a class.

DID YOU UNDERSTAND?

1. The cotton gin/sewing machine/telephone/ typewriter/phonograph/light bulb.
2. They formed labor unions to fight for better hours, better pay, and safer workplaces.
3. The United States needed farmers and workers.

TEXT PAGES 177–179: *20th-Century History*

FOCUS

TOPICS

World War I
The Depression
Franklin Delano Roosevelt
World War II
The United Nations
The Cold War, the Korean War, and the Vietnam War

GRAMMAR

Past Tense

The United States enter**ed** World War II in 1941.
World War I **began** in 1914.
From 1950 to 1953, the United States **fought** in the Korean War.
Roosevelt **was** the President during World War II.
The Depression **had** many causes.

NEW VOCABULARY

Page 177:

Austria- Hungary	cut	lose
bank	Depression	money
borrow	economy	salary
century	Germany	stock market
close	Great	world power
collapse	Depression	World War I
	job	

Page 178:

Allied nations	home	New Deal
atomic bomb	Italy	park
bomb (v.)	Japan	Pearl Harbor
bridge	keep	plan
building	loan	Social Security
drop	make	system
Hiroshima	Nagasaki	World War II

Page 179:

assistance	forces	political
Cold War	health	system
compete	program	provide
discuss	international	United
economic aid	Korean War	Nations (UN)
education	organization	Vietnam War
program	peace	

(These three pages contain six separate stories. Cover each story separately, using the usual teaching steps.)

WORLD WAR I

PREVIEWING THE STORY

Have students talk about the story title and the photograph to establish the context of the story. Ask some or all of the following questions:

> What do these posters say?
> Why were they important?
> Who is Uncle Sam?

READING THE STORY

(See previous chapters for the usual teaching steps for reading the story.)

> *Reading Comprehension Check*
>
> When did World War I begin?
> Who fought in the war?
> When did the United States enter the war?/Who did the United States help?
> When did the war end?
> What did the United States become?

EXPANSION

Have students discuss their own countries' roles in World War I.

THE DEPRESSION

PREVIEWING THE STORY

Have students talk about the story title and the photographs to establish the context of the story. Ask some or all of the following questions:

> Who are the people in the first picture?
> Where do you think they are?
> Describe what kind of life you think they have.

Who are the people in the second picture?
What are they doing?
How do they feel?/What are they thinking?

READING THE STORY

(See previous chapters for the usual teaching steps for reading the story.)

> *Reading Comprehension Check*
>
> When was there a Great Depression?
> What happened to the American economy?
>
> Name one cause of the Depression.
> Name a second cause of the Depression.
> Name a third cause of the Depression.
>
> What kind of time was it in the United States during the Depression?
> What happened at that time?

EXPANSION

Have students discuss a current or past time in their native country when the economy was bad. Have them discuss the causes and effects.

FRANKLIN DELANO ROOSEVELT

PREVIEWING THE STORY

Have students talk about the story title and the photograph to establish the context of the story. Ask some or all of the following questions:

> Who is this man?
> What did he do?

READING THE STORY

(See previous chapters for the usual teaching steps for reading the story.)

> *Reading Comprehension Check*
>
> Who was the president from 1932 to 1945?
> Did Roosevelt become president during good times in the United States?
> What was the New Deal?
> What did the government do for people who had no work?
> What did the people do?
> Why did the government give people loans?
> What system began at this time?
>
> Who was the president during World War II?
> How long did he serve?
> When did he die?

EXPANSION

Have students discuss important leaders in their own countries during times of crisis. Have them describe their countries' problems at those times and how the leader helped the country.

WORLD WAR II

PREVIEWING THE STORY

Have students talk about the story title and the photograph to establish the context of the story. Ask some or all of the following questions:

> Who are these people?
> Where are they?
> What are they doing?

READING THE STORY

(See previous chapters for the usual teaching steps for reading the story.)

> *Reading Comprehension Check*
>
> When did World War II begin?
> Which countries were called the Allied Nations?
> Who did they fight against?
> When did the United States enter World War II?
> What did the United States do in 1945?
> Who won the war? When?

EXPANSION

Have students discuss their own countries' roles in World War II.

THE UNITED NATIONS (THE UN)

PREVIEWING THE STORY

Have students talk about the story title and the photograph to establish the context of the story. Ask some or all of the following questions:

> What is this building?
> Where is it?
> Who works there?
> What do they do?

READING THE STORY

(See previous chapters for the usual teaching steps for reading the story.)

> *Reading Comprehension Check*
>
> What organization did many countries form after World War II?
> What is it also called?

What happens at the United Nations?
Does the United Nations help some countries? How?

EXPANSION

1. Have students discuss the United Nations' role in their native countries.

2. Have students discuss whether the United Nations is an effective organization, giving reasons for their answers.

THE COLD WAR, THE KOREAN WAR, AND THE VIETNAM WAR

PREVIEWING THE STORY

Have students talk about the story title and the photographs to establish the context of the story. Ask some or all of the following questions:

> The first picture shows the Berlin Wall. What two countries did this wall separate? What happened to this wall in 1989 and 1990?
> What were the differences between life on one side of the wall and life on the other?
> What do you see in the second picture?
> What are they doing there?

READING THE STORY

(See previous chapters for the usual teaching steps for reading the story.)

> *Reading Comprehension Check*
>
> Which two countries became world powers after World War II?
> Did they have the same political systems?
> Which system is democratic and which was communist?
> How did they compete?
> What was the *Cold War*?
>
> How many times has the United States fought Communist forces since World War II?
> When did the United States fight in the Korean War?
> What war did the United States fight from 1964 to 1973?
> When did the Cold War end?

EXPANSION

1. Have students discuss current relations between Russia and the United States.

2. Have students discuss the involvement of foreign powers in their native countries.

VOCABULARY CHECK

1. United Nations
2. World War I
3. New Deal
4. Depression
5. Cold War

1. Franklin Delano Roosevelt.
2. Germany, Italy, and Japan.
3. England and Russia.
4. It discusses world problems / helps many countries / gives economic aid / provides education programs, health programs, and other assistance.

DID YOU UNDERSTAND?

Have students provide short answers to these questions.

1. The American economy collapsed. Factories and farms produced too much. / After World War I, countries in Europe didn't have money to buy American goods. / Many people borrowed too much money.
2. President Franklin D. Roosevelt's plan to help the country.
3. In 1941, after the Japanese bombed Pearl Harbor.
4. The American system is democratic, and the Soviet system was communist.
5. The United Nations, an international organization.

FACT CHECK

1. Vietnam
2. Social Security
3. Depression
4. Japan
5. communist

LISTENING

Have students complete the exercises as you play the audio program or read the following:

Listen and circle the correct answer.

1. Who was the president during World War II?
2. When did the United States enter World War II?
3. What two countries became major world powers after World War II?
4. Which countries did the United States fight against during World War II?
5. What new international organization was formed after World War II?
6. What happened during the Depression?

Answers

1. b
2. a
3. b

4. a
5. b
6. a

QUESTIONS AND ANSWERS

This exercise offers students important practice with the multiple ways a question might be posed by the INS examiner. First, have students repeat each question after you. Then, have students practice asking and answering the questions with other students. Finally, have students write their answers to questions 1–4.

FOCUS

TOPICS

The Civil Rights Movement
Martin Luther King, Jr.

GRAMMAR

Past Tense

It work**ed** for equal rights for all Americans.
He **led** protests against discrimination in
  many states.
In 1968 Martin Luther King, Jr., **was** shot
  and killed.

NEW VOCABULARY

civil rights	March on Washington
demonstration	remember
discrimination	shoot
equal rights	support
kill	thousand

PREVIEWING THE STORY

Have students talk about the story title and the
photograph to establish the context of the story. Ask
some or all of the following questions:

Who is this man?
Where is he?
What is he doing?
Who is he talking to?
What do you think he's saying?

READING THE STORY

1. Have students read the story silently.
2. **Check Reading Comprehension:** Ask
   students a question about each line of the story.
   For beginning-level students, ask these questions
   in the order below so that the questions follow
   the sequence of the story. For higher-level
   students, ask the questions in random order.

   What did the civil rights movement work for?
   Whose equal rights did it work for?

   Who was the most famous leader of the civil
     rights movement?
   What did he lead protests against?
   What did he do in 1963?
   What was this called?

   What happened to Martin Luther King, Jr., in
     1968?
   What did the nation lose?
   How does the United States remember Martin
     Luther King, Jr.?

3. Ask students if they have any questions about
   the story; check understanding of vocabulary.
4. **Choral Repetition:** Read aloud each line of the
   story and have students repeat.
5. **Class Circle Reading:** Have students read the
   story aloud as a class, with different students
   reading each line. (You can assign each line to a
   particular student or by seating patterns, or by
   letting students take turns spontaneously. In
   large classes, have a different group or row of
   students read each line.)
6. **Pair Practice:** Have students work in pairs,
   reading the passage to each other paragraph by
   paragraph. Circulate around the room and check
   students' reading and pronunciation, focusing
   more attention on students who need more
   assistance.

TEXT PAGE 183: VOICE OF FREEDOM: *Martin Luther King, Jr.*

(As noted in the text, this lesson is provided for enrichment and speaking practice. It is not required for the INS interview.)

FOCUS

> ### TOPICS
>
> The Civil Rights Movement
> Martin Luther King, Jr.
>
> ### GRAMMAR
>
> **Future: Will**
>
> One day this nation **will** rise up.
>
> **Must**
>
> If America is to be a great nation this **must** become true.

NEW VOCABULARY

> beautiful
> part
> powerful

READING THE STORY

1. Have students read the introductory sentences silently.

2. **Check Reading Comprehension:** Ask students questions about the introduction.

   What year was the *March on Washington?* Who gave a famous speech there? Where? What is this speech called?

3. **Listening:** With books closed, have students listen to the introduction and the excerpt in the box—presented by you or on the audio program.

4. **Reading:** Have students read along silently as they listen to the passage again—presented by you or on the audio program.

5. **Choral Reading:** Have students read the passage aloud in unison, along with you or the audio program.

6. Ask students if they understand the general meaning of the passage. (They do not need to know the exact meaning of unfamiliar words.)

7. **Public Speaking Practice:** Have individual students present the excerpted passage to the class. If you feel it is appropriate to do so, help students with their diction and projection to improve their public speaking skills in English.

8. **Pair Practice:** Have students work in pairs, taking turns reading the passage to each other. Circulate around the room and check students' reading and pronunciation, focusing more attention on students who need more assistance.

DISCUSSION

Have students discuss both questions in pairs or small groups and then share as a class.

1. Have students discuss how the accomplishments of the civil rights movement help them today. Talk about fair housing, equal opportunities in employment and education, and so on.

2. Have students discuss whether there is still discrimination in the United States today and give reasons for their answers.

EXPANSION

1. Have an oratorical contest. Have interested students memorize the excerpt of the speech and present it to the class. Have class members vote on the best rendition, and award a prize to the winner.

2. Many libraries have videos, movies, or audio recordings of the actual "I Have a Dream" speech. Play the speech for students and have them discuss its meaning and importance.

3. Have students share their own dreams of what kind of nation or what kind of world there should be.

TEXT PAGE 184: *Citizens' Rights and Responsibilities*

FOCUS

> **TOPIC**
>
> Citizens' Rights and Responsibilities
>
> **GRAMMAR**
>
> **Can**
>
> Citizens **can** vote for federal, state, and local officials.
>
> **Should**
>
> Citizens **should** know what is happening in their city.

NEW VOCABULARY

active	happen	radio
candidate	jury	Republican
choose	news	responsibility
community	newspaper	should
Democratic	obey	television
follow	party	usually

PREVIEWING THE STORY

Have students talk about the story title, the photograph, and the illustration to establish the context of the story. Ask some or all of the following questions:

> What is the man in the first picture doing?
> Where is he?
> How do people vote in your native country?
> Who are the people in the second picture?
> Where are they?
> What are they doing?
> Have you ever gone to court in the United States?

READING THE STORY

1. Have students read the story silently.

2. **Check Reading Comprehension:** Ask students a question about each line of the story. For beginning-level students, ask these questions in the order below, so that the questions follow the sequence of the story. For higher-level students, ask the questions in random order.

> What is the most important right U.S. citizens have?
> Who can citizens vote for?
> How often can they vote for the president?
> What two candidates do they usually choose between?
> What are the two major political parties in the United States?
>
> What are some responsibilities citizens have?
> What should citizens know about?
> How should they find out what is happening?

3. Ask students if they have any questions about the story; check understanding of vocabulary.

4. **Choral Repetition:** Read aloud each line of the story and have students repeat.

5. **Class Circle Reading:** Have students read the story aloud as a class, with different students reading each line. (You can assign each line to a particular student or by seating patterns, or by letting students take turns spontaneously. In large classes, have a different group or row of students read each line.)

6. **Pair Practice:** Have students work in pairs, reading the passage to each other paragraph by paragraph. Circulate around the room and check students' reading and pronunciation, focusing more attention on students who need more assistance.

EXPANSION

1. Have students discuss where people vote in their neighborhoods and where people can register to vote.

2. Have students discuss how they feel on Election Day when they cannot vote. How will they feel different when they become citizens and they can vote?

3. Invite a member of the League of Women Voters or a similar organization to speak to the class about being informed citizens.

FOCUS

TOPIC

Presidents: 1961 to Present

GRAMMAR

Past Tense

He work**ed** for civil rights.
He **didn't** have experience in national politics.
Richard Nixon **was** the President from 1969 to 1974.
He **took** office after President Nixon resigned.
He **became** the president in 2001.

NEW VOCABULARY

acquit	Operation Desert
actor	Storm
administration	organization
Afghanistan	peace-keeping
bad	mission
Bosnia	policy
count	poor
create	recession
drugs	reform(v.)
eliminate	relation
experience	resign
foreign	role
former	scandal
Great Society	send
Gulf War	son
human rights	spending
impeach	terrorist organization
impeachment trial	unusual
improve	volunteer
international terrorist	Watergate
Kosovo	welfare system
lower (v.)	World Trade Center
office	young(est)

(These four pages contain nine separate stories. Cover each story separately, using the usual teaching steps.)

PREVIEWING THE STORIES

For each reading passage, ask some or all of the following questions:

Who is this man?
What do you know about him?
Is he still alive?

READING THE STORY

(See previous chapters for the usual teaching steps for reading the stories. Questions for checking reading comprehension are included below.)

John F. Kennedy

When was John F. Kennedy the president?
Was he the youngest U.S. president?
What did he work for?
Who did he want to help?
Where did he send soldiers?
What happened in 1963?

Lyndon B. Johnson

When was Lyndon B. Johnson the president?
When did he become president?
What was the Great Society?
What laws were passed during his administration?
What war expanded during his administration?

Richard Nixon

When was Richard Nixon the president?
With what country did he begin relations?
What did he end?
Why did he resign?

Gerald Ford

When was Gerald Ford the president?
Was he elected?
When did he take office?
How was the economy during his time in office?

James Earl (Jimmy) Carter

When was Jimmy Carter the president?
What did he work for?
Did he have experience in national politics?
How was the economy during his time in office?

Ronald Reagan

When was Ronald Reagan the president?
What did he do?
What happened to the role of the federal government during his time in office?
How was the economy during his time in office?
What did Ronald Reagan do before he entered politics?
What was he called as president?

George Bush

When was George Bush the president?
What did he do before he became the president?
What did he do with many of the Reagan
    policies?
How was the economy during his time in office?
Where did he send soldiers in 1991?
How many terms did he serve?

William J. (Bill) Clinton

When was Bill Clinton the president?
What happened to taxes, government spending,
    and the national debt during his time in
    office?
What did he increase federal money for?
Where did he send troops? Why?
What kind of scandals was he involved in?
In what year was he impeached by the House of
    Representatives?
What happened in the Senate a year later?
Did President Clinton stay in office?

George W. Bush

Who is the father of George W. Bush?
When did George W. Bush become the president?
Why was the election very unusual?
What happened on September 11, 2001?
Where did President Bush send troops? Why?

EXPANSION

1. Have students discuss who their favorite U.S.
   president is and give reasons for their answers.

2. Have students discuss whether they think the
   president today is doing a good job and give
   reasons for their answers.

TEXT PAGE 189: *September 11, 2001*

FOCUS

TOPIC

September 11, 2001

GRAMMAR

Past Tense

Terrorists hijack**ed** four airplanes.
Most of the victims **were** Americans.
He **sent** American troops there.

NEW VOCABULARY

Afghanistan	Pentagon
air attack	responsible
airplane	terrorism
attack	terrorist
collapse	terrorist
crash (v.)	organization
headquarters	twin towers
hijack	victim
order (v.)	World Trade Center

PREVIEWING THE STORY

Have students talk about the story title and the
television images to establish the context of the
story. Ask some or all of the following questions:

What do you see on the TV screen on the left?
    Where is this? When did this happen?
What do you see on the TV screen on the right?
    Where is this? When did this happen?
Where were you, and what were you doing, when
    this happened?
What was your reaction? What were you
    thinking and feeling?

READING THE STORY

1. Have students read the story silently.

2. **Check Reading Comprehension:** Ask
   students a question about each line of the story.
   For beginning-level students, ask these questions
   in the order below so that the questions follow
   the sequence of the story. For higher-level
   students, ask the questions in random order.

   Who hijacked four airplanes on the morning
       of September 11, 2001, and where?
   Where did the hijackers crash two planes in
       New York City?
   What happened to the twin towers of the
       World Trade Center?

Where did one plane crash in Virginia?

Where did the fourth plane crash?

How many people died?

How many countries were they from?

Who were most of the victims?

What did the U.S. government ask other nations to do?

What did President Bush order?

Where did he send American troops?

3. Ask students if they have any questions about the story; check understanding of vocabulary.

(Note: Given the content of this reading passage, please refrain from the usual Choral Repetition practice.)

4. **Class Circle Reading:** Have students read the story aloud as a class, with different students reading each line. (You can assign each line to a particular student or by seating patterns, or by letting students take turns spontaneously. In large classes, have a different group or row of students read each line.)

5. **Pair Practice:** Have students work in pairs, reading the passage to each other paragraph by paragraph. Circulate around the room and check students' reading and pronunciation, focusing more attention on students who need more assistance.

EXPANSION

1. If you saved newspapers or magazine articles covering the events of September 11, 2001, bring them to class to share with students.

2. Have students discuss if they think the United States or the world changed on that day, and in what ways.

3. Encourage students to share any personal stories about their reaction to the events or experiences they had related to the events. (Students commonly share feelings ranging from fear and concern to pride and identification with the United States. Their experiences might include accounts of economic difficulties or discrimination after the events, or accounts of community commemorations they attended or other events that helped make them feel a part of the community.)

TEXT PAGE 190: *Check-Up*

EVENTS IN HISTORY

1. March on Washington
2. Watergate
3. Great Society
4. Gulf War
5. House of Representatives

PEOPLE IN HISTORY

1. Richard Nixon
2. John F. Kennedy
3. Martin Luther King, Jr.
4. George W. Bush
5. Bill Clinton

DID YOU UNDERSTAND?

Have students provide short answers to these questions.

1. It was a movement during the 1950s and 1960s that worked to end discrimination against Blacks in the United States.
2. Martin Luther King, Jr.
3. Lyndon B. Johnson.
4. Richard Nixon.
5. Ronald Reagan.

TEXT PAGE 191: INTERVIEW: *I'm Not Sure I Understand the Question*

FOCUS

TOPICS

Citizens' Rights and Responsibilities
The Civil Rights Movement
World War II

GRAMMAR

Can

And **can** you tell me who Martin Luther King, Jr., was?

Past Tense

Which countries **did** we fight with in World War II?
Who **were** the Allies?

FUNCTIONAL INTERVIEW SKILLS

Reporting Information
Clarifying Ambiguous Questions

NEW VOCABULARY

Allies	Do you mean . . .
enemy	I'm not sure . . .
grant	
ready	

PRACTICING THE DIALOG

1. **Setting the Scene:** Have students look at the photo and determine who is talking: an INS examiner and an applicant. Establish the context: "The INS examiner is asking questions about the government and U.S. history."

2. **Listening:** With books closed, have students listen to the dialog—presented by you, by a pair of students, or on the audio program.

3. **Choral Repetition:** With books still closed, model each line and have the whole class repeat in unison.

4. **Reading:** With books open, have students follow along as two students present the dialog. Ask students if they have any questions and check understanding of vocabulary.

5. **Choral Conversation Practice:** Divide the class in half. Have Group 1 ask the questions and Group 2 give the answers; then reverse. (Or: You ask the questions and have the whole class answer in unison; then reverse.)

6. Call on one or two pairs of students to present the dialog.

7. **Pair Practice:** Have students practice the dialog in pairs, taking turns being the INS examiner and the applicant.

8. Call on one or two more pairs of students to present the dialog to the class.

Dialog Note:

Line 10: The applicant is not sure what the examiner's question means. Rather than guessing at the meaning, the applicant asks the examiner to clarify the question. Students should request clarification whenever possible in such situations.

> A. Are you ready for some questions about history and government?
> B. Yes, I am.
> A. Okay. What are the two major political parties in the United States today?
> B. The *Democratic Party* and the *Republican Party*.
> A. What's the most important right granted to U.S. citizens?
> B. *The right to vote.*
> A. And can you tell me who Martin Luther King, Jr., was?
> B. Yes. He was *the leader of the civil rights movement.*
> A. Which countries did we fight with in World War II?
> B. I'm sorry. I'm not sure I understand the question. Do you mean which countries were our enemies, or which countries did we help?
> A. Who did we help? Who were the Allies?
> B. *England and Russia.*
> A. Good. And can you tell me who the president was during World War II?
> B. Yes. It was *Franklin Delano Roosevelt.*

Point out to students that this review activity contains twelve pairs of questions. During an INS interview, the examiner may follow one question with another related question. These exercises offer students practice with such followup questions.

First have students write the answers to the questions on a separate sheet of paper. Then have them work in pairs, asking and answering the questions (one at a time). Students can provide long or short answers to these questions.

1. Labor Day.

   It celebrates the workers of the United States.

2. Because all Americans except Native Americans come from families of immigrants.

   Some immigrants come here because life was difficult or dangerous in their native country. Others come here because they want a better life for themselves and their families.

3. The Great Depression was the time from 1929 to 1939 when the American economy collapsed.

   Factories closed, workers lost their jobs or their salaries were cut, many banks closed, and many people lost all their money in the stock market.

4. Franklin Delano Roosevelt.

   The government made jobs for people who had no work. The government gave people loans to help them keep their farms or homes. The Social Security system began.

5. In 1941.

   Germany, Italy, and Japan.

6. The United Nations, an international organization.

   Countries discuss world problems and try to keep peace. The UN also helps many countries with economic aid, education programs, health programs, and other assistance.

7. The United States and the Soviet Union.

   The American system is democratic, and the Soviet system was communist.

8. Martin Luther King, Jr., Day.

   It celebrates the most famous leader of the civil rights movement.

9. Citizens should vote, obey the laws, pay taxes, serve on a jury, and be active in their communities.

   The right to vote.

10. Richard Nixon.

    He resigned because of a political scandal called Watergate.

11. Bill Clinton.

    He was involved in political and personal scandals.

12. Terrorists attacked the World Trade Center in New York City and the Pentagon in Arlington, Virginia.

    George W. Bush.

TEXT PAGE 193: Review

TALKING TIME LINE: *Important Dates in U.S. History*

Have students complete the time line. Then have them work in pairs, asking and answering the questions at the end of the exercise based on the information recorded on the time line.

1917	The United States entered World War I.
1929	The Great Depression began in the United States.
1941	Japan bombed Pearl Harbor.
1945	World War II ended.
1963	Martin Luther King, Jr., led a civil rights march in Washington.
1998	The House of Representatives impeached President Clinton.
2001	Terrorists attacked the World Trade Center and the Pentagon.

TEXT PAGES 194–195: *Chapter Test*

You can use this test as a standardized form of assessment to measure student achievement of the curriculum objectives in Chapter 10. The test consists of 20 multiple-choice items and five sentences for dictation.

To score the test on a scale of 100:

- For each correct multiple-choice item, score four points.

- For each dictation sentence, do a general evaluation of the correctness of words, spelling, punctuation, and legibility. Score each sentence as follows:

    4 (Excellent), **3** (Good), **2** (Fair), **1** (Poor), **0** (Unsatisfactory)

Students can write their answers in the text or on the reproducible Chapter Test Answer Sheet provided in the Appendix.

A. COMPLETE THE SENTENCES

1. C
2. D
3. B
4. B
5. D
6. A
7. B
8. B
9. A
10. C
11. C
12. D

B. ANSWER THE QUESTIONS

13. A
14. C
15. D
16. C
17. B
18. D
19. A
20. D

C. DICTATION

Have students write these sentences as you read each sentence twice or play the audio program:

1. The first Americans were farmers.

2. Many factory workers got hurt.

3. Immigrants came from many different countries.

4. The United States has a democratic system of government.

5. The most important right citizens have is the right to vote.

PERFORMANCE-BASED ASSESSMENT

These civics enrichment activities are designed to promote students' active participation in class and in the civic life of the community—through projects, issues discussions, community tasks, field trips, and Internet activities. Reproducible performance-based assessment forms for use in evaluating and documenting student participation in these activities are included in the Appendix.

CIVIC PARTICIPATION

Election Day in your community: Have students discuss where polling places are located in your community. Ask them to describe what happens at the polling places on Election Day. If they can, have students describe what voting machines look like, what local officials people vote for in your community, and how people register to vote. Have students obtain information from the local Board of Elections about registering and voting. If your class term coincides with an Election Day, try to arrange a visit to a polling place with your students.

PROJECT ACTIVITY

Biography Project: Have students work individually on a short biography about a famous American—an inventor, a president, or someone else. Help students brainstorm as a class a list of possible subjects for their biographies. Accompany students to your school library or a local library to find information about their subjects. Introduce students to some basic library skills for locating information. Have students submit first drafts of their biographies and then meet with you to discuss your feedback and corrections. Then have them submit final versions, and display these on a bulletin board. Students should give short presentations to the class about the subjects of their biographies.

COMMUNITY ISSUES

Problem-Posing Discussion: Have students discuss the rights and responsibilities of all people in their communities and in the nation. Have them explore how these rights and responsibilities may differ for citizens and non-citizens. As students identify key issues and problems, have them share ideas about how to solve them.

TECHNOLOGY ENRICHMENT

See Appendix page 161 for additional Internet enrichment activities related to this chapter.

APPENDIX

TEXT PAGES 199–203: *100 Questions for Review*

INS examiners often use some of the 100 questions (or ones similar to them) found on pages 199–203 in their interviews of naturalization applicants. The questions are listed here in two columns so that students can cover up the answers and test themselves. Students should also practice asking and answering these questions in pairs.

TEXT PAGES 204–206: *Songs of Freedom*

1. **Choral Repetition:** Read aloud each line of the song and have students repeat in unison.

2. **Listening to the Song:** Have students listen to the song by playing the audio or singing it yourself.

3. **Singing Aloud:** Play the instrumental version of the song and have students sing along. (The instrumental version follows the vocal version on the audio program.)

TEXT PAGE 207: *Words of Freedom*

PLEDGE OF ALLEGIANCE

(Note: You may want to have students stand and place their right hands on their chests while practicing the Pledge in parts or in its entirety.)

1. **Choral Repetition (phrase by phrase):** Read aloud each phrase and have students repeat in unison.

2. **Reading:** Have students practice reading the Pledge as a class, in small groups, or on their own.

3. **Reciting**: Have students memorize the Pledge and practice reciting it as a class, in small groups, and on their own.

OATH OF ALLEGIANCE

(Note: Explain to students that new citizens recite this oath of allegiance to the United States at their naturalization ceremony. It is not necessary for students to memorize the oath.)

1. **Choral Repetition (phrase by phrase):** Read aloud the Oath of Allegiance phrase by phrase and have students repeat in unison.

2. **Reading:** Have students practice reading the Oath of Allegiance as a class, in small groups, or on their own.

TEACHER'S
RESOURCES

Teacher's Resources

Technology Enrichment: Websites for Internet Activities

Needs Assessment Forms
    Pictorial Version
    Checklist Version

Pre-Post Assessments
    Pre-Post Assessment 1 (Chapters A, B, 1, 2, 3)
    Pre-Post Assessment 2 (Chapters 4, 5, 6, 7)
    Pre-Post Assessment 3 (Chapters 8, 9, 10)
    Pre-Post Assessment Answer Keys

Performance-Based Assessment Records
    Student Name List Mask
    Assessment Records (for each chapter)
    Project Activity Observation Checklist

Chapter Test Answer Sheet

The INS Interview: Information for Students

English & Civics Instruction Resources

Correlation Key

The resources in this section are designed as tools for effective instruction, assessment, and documentation of student progress. These materials may be reproduced for classroom use.

A *Technology Enrichment* section provides a list of websites for additional Internet activities that expand upon the topics in each chapter.

Needs Assessment Forms are designed to help programs or instructors gather input from students about their needs and interests in order to guide the development of instruction. A Pictorial Version provides a simple format for low-beginning-level students; a Checklist Version offers a more detailed format for students who have some reading ability.

Pre-Post Assessments are knowledge/skill surveys that may be used to evaluate students' prior knowledge and abilities before instruction as well as student achievement of learning objectives after instruction. Three pre-post assessments are provided, one for each third of the *Voices of Freedom* instructional program.

Performance-Based Assessment Records provide tools for evaluating and documenting student participation and performance in each chapter's Civics Enrichment activities, which are designed to promote students' active participation in class and in the civic life of the community. Scoring rubrics guide the alternative assessment of these projects, issues discussions, community tasks, field trips, and Internet activities.

The Student Name List Mask provides a convenient way to make a list of students' names and then affix it to each of the Assessment Record forms. The Project Activity Observation Checklist provides an assessment tool for evaluating students as they participate in all phases of a project and develop skills in leadership, teamwork, and communicating information—key workplace skills identified by the Secretary's Commission on Achieving Necessary Skills (SCANS).

The *Chapter Test Answer Sheet* offers a means for students to record their test answers on a sheet that can be handed in. Space is provided for students to bubble in their answers to the twenty multiple-choice questions and to write the five dictation sentences in each test. Using this, students practice the coordination skills involved in matching questions in a test booklet with the corresponding answer lines on a separate answer sheet.

The *INS Interview: Information for Students* section offers students helpful advice about what to expect at an INS interview and important practice with the types of questions about personal information and other topics that they may need to answer.

English & Civics Instruction Resources include listings of websites, print resources, and videos that provide background information and instructional materials.

A *Correlation Key* indicates how to integrate the civics instruction in *Voices of Freedom* with the language instruction offered in *Side by Side, Foundations, Word by Word, Access,* and *ExpressWays.*

Technology Enrichment: Websites for Internet Activities

These websites can be accessed directly through the Longman English Literacy (EL)/Civics homepage at http://www.longman.com/ae/elcivics.html.

CHAPTER 1

http://www.jayzeebear.com/map/usa.html
A map of the United States appears without the names of the states. Students can move the mouse cursor over the states and then the names appear. After students practice, they can play games to test their knowledge of the U.S. map.

http://www.niehs.nih.gov/kids/lyrics/america.htm
This website offers the lyrics and music of *America the Beautiful*. Students can read the lyrics and sing along.

CHAPTER 2

http://www.ushistory.org/betsy/index.html
The Betsy Ross Homepage gives information about the woman who sewed the first American flag. It also gives instructions on how to display the flag, and it includes drawings to show how the flag appeared at different times in U.S. history. You can use this website to create an online scavenger hunt for students. Browse the site, find pieces of information in different locations, and write a list of questions for students to answer by locating the information.

http://www.ushistory.org/documents/pledge.htm
Students can read the words to the original Pledge of Allegiance written by Francis Bellamy in 1892, and they can learn about the changes to the Pledge of Allegiance over the years.

http://www.link4u.com/pledge.htm
This presentation in words and music describes the meaning of the Pledge of Allegiance.

http://www.link4u.com/onenation.htm
This website features a country song about the Pledge of Allegiance.

CHAPTER 3

http://www.senate.gov/
Students can visit their state senators online at this official website of the U.S. Senate. (Students visit their representative's website in the Civics Enrichment activity on page 70.) Have students describe the kind of information they find.

CHAPTER 4

http://www.supremecourtus.gov/about/photos.html
The official website of the U.S. Supreme Court includes photographs of the Supreme Court building. Ask students the following questions, which they can answer by locating information at this website: What are the names of the two statues at the entrance of the Supreme Court building? Where do the Supreme Court justices meet to discuss cases? Where did the Supreme Court sit (meet) from 1860 to 1935?

CHAPTER 5

http://www.firstgov.gov/
This website is the U.S. government's official web portal. Students can click in the menu at the left to visit online the different agencies at the federal, state, and local levels of government. Have students use this website, or other websites for your state and local governments, to find information about driver's licenses, public schools, garbage collection, parks, and other services. As a class, brainstorm all the other information students might want to know about life in their community or in their state, and identify websites where this information can be found online.

CHAPTER 6

www.infoplease.com/states.html
This website features information about each state, including the state capital, population, history, flag, economy, and places of interest. Students can use the information as they complete their report on one of the states—the social studies enrichment activity on page 111.

http://www.thanksgivingrecipe.com/default.asp
This website provides Thanksgiving recipes. Have students browse the site, choose interesting recipes, and perhaps prepare them for the classroom Thanksgiving celebration suggested on page 116.

http://www.historyisfun.org/jyf1/js.html
This website describes the Jamestown Settlement in Virginia, which is featured on page 113. Ask students the following questions, which they can answer by locating information at this website: What was the name of the native people who lived there? What were the names of the three ships that the colonists sailed to Jamestown? How many colonists arrived on those ships in 1607?

CHAPTER 7

http://chnm.gmu.edu/declaration/
This website provides translations of the Declaration of Independence in Spanish and several other languages. Students can read the document in the native language in order to better understand its meaning and significance in the history of the United States.

http://gi.grolier.com/presidents/ea/quickfac/03fjeff.html
Brief facts about the life of Thomas Jefferson are featured. Ask students the following questions, which they can answer by locating information at this website: When was Thomas Jefferson born? When did he die? Where is he buried? What were his professions before he was the president? How many years did he serve as president?

CHAPTER 8

http://www.archives.gov/exhibit_hall/charters_of_freedom/constitution/constitution_transcription.html
This website offers the complete transcript of the U.S. Constitution and the amendments. Have students notice how the Constitution is organized into articles and sections. Ask them why the following articles and sections are important:
Article 1 Section 2 (established the House of Representatives)
Article 1 Section 3 (established the Senate)
Article 2 Section 1 (established the office of President)
Article 3 Section 1 (established the Supreme Court)

http://memory.loc.gov/const/bor.html
Students can read the entire Bill of Rights. Have students work in pairs or groups and try to understand the meaning of the 2nd though 10th amendments. Then discuss these amendments as a class.

CHAPTER 9

http://www.treefort.org/~rgrogan/web/usa1.htm
This website offers the lyrics and music of the *Star-Spangled Banner*. Students can read the lyrics and sing along.

http://xroads.virginia.edu/~MAP/terr_hp.html
Maps show the expansion of the United States during the period 1775 to 1920. Students can click on the different years and see how the United States grew through expansion.

http://www.nps.gov/liho/home/home.htm
This National Park Service website offers a virtual tour of Abraham Lincoln's home in Springfield, Illinois. Students can take the tour and describe what they see.

Chapter 10

http://educate.si.edu/spotlight/inventors1.html
This Smithsonian Institution website provides information about famous American inventors. Students can choose an inventor, use the hypertext links to go to other sites about the topic, and then report what they learn to the class.

http://www.americanparknetwork.com/parkinfo/sl/index.html
This website about the Statue of Liberty and Ellis Island has a wealth of information about immigration. You can use this website to create an online scavenger hunt for students based on their interests, their backgrounds, and their reading ability. Browse the site, find pieces of information in different locations, and write a list of questions for students to answer by locating the information.

http://www.whitehouse.gov/history/presidents/
This official White House website provides information about all past presidents of the United States. Students can browse the information, choose a president who interests them, and report about the president to the class.

Pictorial Version

Student's Name _____	I.D. Number _____
Course _____ Teacher _____	Date _____

I want to use English at the _____.

___ bank

___ bus station

___ clinic

___ clothing store

___ drug store

___ library

___ post office

___ shopping mall

___ supermarket

_____ _____ _____

NEEDS ASSESSMENT
Pictorial Version

Student's Name _____

I want to learn English to _____.

___ talk with people

___ find an apartment

___ get a job

___ read English books

___ read the newspaper

___ write in English

___ use money

___ use a computer

___ _____

I want to learn about _____.

___ the government of
the United States

___ the history of
the United States

___ _____

Voices of Freedom
Needs Assessment (Pictoral Version)

NEEDS ASSESSMENT
Checklist Version

Student's Name _____	I.D. Number _____
Course _____ Teacher _____	Date _____

I want to use English at the _____ .

____ bank	____ clinic
____ supermarket	____ drug store
____ post office	____ hospital
____ library	____ INS office
____ bus or train station	____ social security office
____ clothing store	____ welfare office
____ department store	____ _____
____ shopping mall	____ _____

- -

I want to learn English to _____ .

____ talk to my neighbors	____ get a job
____ talk to people at my children's school	____ get a better job
____ talk to people at my church/temple/mosque	____ use a computer
____ talk to my building manager	____ use a checkbook
____ talk to the police	____ get a loan
____ use the telephone	____ get a driver's license
____ report emergencies (call 911)	____ report housing repair problems
____ become a citizen	____ use local government services
____ use money	____ understand and speak at school meetings
____ find an apartment	____ understand and speak at local government meetings
____ get job training	____ _____

- -

I want to learn to read in English _____ .

____ books	____ stories to read to my children
____ newspapers	____ the driver's manual
____ magazines	____ want ads
____ advertisements (ads)	____ business letters
____ safety signs	____ pay checks and pay stubs
____ road signs	____ E-mail
____ bills	____ online information (on the World Wide Web)
____ labels	____ warranties (guarantees) on things I buy
____ schedules	____ insurance policies
____ maps	____ contracts and rental agreements/leases
____ letters from school	____ _____
____ report cards from school	

Student's Name _____

I want to learn to write in English to _____.

____ fill out forms	____ pay taxes
____ write letters	____ _____
____ write E-mail messages	____ _____
____ write notes to my children's teachers	____ _____

- -

I want to learn about _____.

____ the government of the United States	____ career options
____ the history of the United States	____ education options
____ holidays in the United States	____ _____
____ culture and attitudes in the United States	____ _____

- -

I want to talk about and solve problems about _____.

____ my neighborhood	____ discrimination/prejudice
____ transportation	____ my workplace/job
____ crime	____ housing
____ alcohol or drugs	____ _____
____ domestic violence	____ _____
____ children or teenagers	____ _____

- -

What else do you want to learn?

_____

_____

_____

_____

_____

_____

_____

Student's Name _____	I.D. Number _____
Course _____ Teacher _____	Date _____

A. CIVICS QUESTIONS

1. What's your full name?

   _____

2. What's your home telephone number? (Include area code.)

   _____

3. What's your address? (Include city, state, and zip code.)

   _____

4. What's your nationality?

   _____

5. In what city or town were you born?

   _____

6. What's your date of birth?

   _____

7. Name the capital of the United States.

   _____

8. What's the capital of your state?

   _____

9. What are the colors of the American flag?

   _____

10. How many stars are there on the American flag?

    _____

11. How many stripes are there on the flag? Why?

    _____

12. What are the names of the three branches of government in the United States?

    _____

13. What building does the President live and work in?

    _____

Student's Name _____

14. Which branch of the government makes the laws?

_____

15. Who works in this branch of the government?

_____

16. Which branch of the government enforces the laws?

_____

17. Who works in this branch of the government?

_____

18. Which branch of the government do the Supreme Court justices work in?

_____

19. What does this branch of the government do?

_____

20. Who works in the U.S. Congress? What building do they work in?

_____

B. WRITING SAMPLE

Answer one of the following questions on a separate sheet of paper.

- Write about the people in your family. What are their names? Where are they?
- Write about your native country. Where is it? What is north, south, east, and west of your native country? What's the name of the capital, and where is it? Where are you from?
- What do the words *freedom* and *democracy* mean to you? Explain.
- Describe the flag of your native country. What are the colors? What's on it?
- Describe the government in your native country. Does it have different branches? What are they called? What are the names and locations of important government buildings? Who are the leaders of the government? Who makes the laws?

Score: **A. Civics Questions:** _____ correct x **4** points   _____ (80)

      B. Writing Sample:
      For each of the following criteria, score **4** (Excellent), **3** (Good), **2** (Fair), **1** (Poor), or **0** (Unsatisfactory).

          Appropriateness of content: _____

          Spelling: _____

          Punctuation & Capitalization: _____

          Grammar: _____

          Completeness of Sentences: _____   _____ (20)

                                                 Total: _____ (100)

| Student's Name _____ | I.D. Number _____ |
| Course _____ Teacher _____ | Date _____ |

A. CIVICS QUESTIONS

1. What are the two parts of the Congress called?

_____

2. How many judges are there in the Supreme Court? Who appoints them?

_____

3. How many U.S. senators are there? How long is a senator's term?

_____

4. How many U.S. representatives are there? How long is a representative's term?

_____

5. What are the three levels of government in the United States?

_____

6. What is the head of a state's government called?

_____

7. What is the U.S. Constitution? What does it do?

_____

8. How many amendments are there to the Constitution? What are the first 10 amendments called?

_____

9. Name four rights guaranteed by the 1st Amendment to the Constitution.

_____

10. Where was the first American colony? What country were the colonists from?

_____

11. Why did the Pilgrims come to America? What was the name of their ship?

_____

12. Who helped the Pilgrims in America? How?

_____

13. What holiday did the Pilgrims celebrate in the fall of 1621? How did they celebrate?

_____

Student's Name _____

14. What were the original states called? How many original states were there?

_____

15. Why did the American colonies fight against England during the Revolutionary War?

_____

16. Who was the leader of the Colonial Army during the Revolutionary War?

_____

17. On what date did the colonists declare their independence? Where?

_____

18. What is the basic belief of the Declaration of Independence?

_____

19. Who wrote the Declaration of Independence?

_____

20. What national holiday do Americans celebrate on July 4th?

_____

B. WRITING SAMPLE

Answer one of the following questions on a separate sheet of paper.

- What are the three branches of government in the United States? What does each branch do? Who works in each branch? How long do they serve?
- Why is the Bill of Rights important?
- Write about your journey to the United States. When did you leave your native country? Why? How? Where did you arrive in the United States? What did you do?
- What kind of taxes do people pay in the United States? What is this money used for?
- Was there a revolutionary war in your native country? When? Write about it.

Score: **A. Civics Questions:** _____ correct x **4** points   _____ (80)

            (Give 1/2 credit if one part of a two-part question is correct.)

      B. Writing Sample:
      For each of the following criteria, score **4** (Excellent), **3** (Good), **2** (Fair), **1** (Poor), or **0** (Unsatisfactory).

            Appropriateness of content: _____

            Spelling: _____

            Punctuation & Capitalization: _____

            Grammar: _____

            Completeness of Sentences: _____   _____ (20)

                                                  Total: _____ (100)

Student's Name		I.D. Number
Course	Teacher	Date

A. CIVICS QUESTIONS

1. What is the Constitution of the United States? What did it establish?

2. What is the Bill of Rights? What does it do?

3. Where was the Constitutional Convention in 1787? Who was its leader?

4. What is the national anthem of the United States? Who wrote it?

5. Why did the United States expand in the 1800s?

6. What are the 49th and 50th states of the Union?

7. What was the Civil War? When did it happen?

8. Who was the president during the Civil War? Why was he important?

9. What are changes in the Constitution called? How many are there?

10. Name an important invention during the Industrial Revolution.

11. Why did workers form labor unions?

12. Why did the United States need immigrants during the 1800s?

13. What happened during the Great Depression?

Student's Name _____

14. Which president had a plan called The New Deal? What happened under this plan?

   _____

15. Which countries did the United States fight against during World War II?

   _____

16. What is the United Nations?

   _____

17. Which two major countries competed during the Cold War? How were they different?

   _____

18. What did the civil rights movement do? Who was its most famous leader?

   _____

19. What is the most important right U.S. citizens have?

   _____

20. What happened on September 11, 2001?

   _____

B. WRITING SAMPLE

Answer one of the following questions on a separate sheet of paper.

- What was one main cause of the Civil War? Explain.
- Write about three important amendments to the Constitution. Why are they important?
- Why is the United States called "a nation of immigrants"? Explain.
- Write about a president of the United States. What did this president do? What happened during this president's time in office?
- Write about your reaction to the events on September 11, 2001. What were you thinking and feeling?

Score: **A. Civics Questions:** _____ correct x **4** points   _____ (80)

   B. Writing Sample:
   For each of the following criteria, score **4** (Excellent), **3** (Good), **2** (Fair), **1** (Poor), or **0** (Unsatisfactory).

   Appropriateness of content: _____

   Spelling: _____

   Punctuation & Capitalization: _____

   Grammar: _____

   Completeness of Sentences: _____   _____ (20)

                                        Total: _____ (100)

PRE-POST ASSESSMENT ANSWER KEYS

Pre-Post Assessment 1

1. (Student's full name.)
2. (Student's home telephone number, including area code.)
3. (Student's address, including city, state, and zip code.)
4. (Student's nationality.)
5. (Student's city or town of birth.)
6. (Student's date of birth.)
7. Washington, D.C.
8. (Name of state capital.)
9. Red, white, and blue.
10. Fifty (50).
11. Thirteen (13). There is one stripe for each of the first thirteen states. / There is one stripe for each of the colonies.
12. The legislative, executive, and judicial branches.
13. The White House.
14. The legislative branch.
15. Senators and representatives.
16. The executive branch.
17. The president and the vice president.
18. The judicial branch.
19. It explains the laws.
20. Senators and representatives. They work in the Capitol.

Pre-Post Assessment 2

1. The Senate and the House of Representatives.
2. Nine (9). The president.
3. One hundred (100). Six (6) years.
4. 435. Two (2) years.
5. Federal, state, and local.
6. The governor.
7. The supreme law of the land. It gives the rules for the three branches of government. / It says what each branch of the government can do and what each branch can't do.
8. Twenty-seven (27). The Bill of Rights.
9. Freedom of speech, freedom of the press, freedom of religion, freedom of assembly.
10. In Jamestown, Virginia. From England.
11. They wanted religious freedom. The Mayflower.
12. The Native Americans. They taught the Pilgrims how to grow corn and other food. / They taught the Pilgrims how to fish. / They helped the Pilgrims build houses.
13. Thanksgiving. They had a big dinner.
14. Colonies. Thirteen (13).
15. The colonies didn't like English taxes, they didn't like English laws, and they didn't have any representatives in England. / The colonies wanted to be independent.
16. George Washington.
17. July 4, 1776. (At Independence Hall) in Philadelphia.
18. All people are created equal.
19. Thomas Jefferson.
20. Independence Day.

Pre-Post Assessment 3

1. The supreme law of the land. It established the form of government in the United States. / It established three branches of government.
2. The first ten amendments to the Constitution. The Bill of Rights gives rights and freedoms to all people in the United States.
3. In Philadelphia. George Washington.
4. The Star-Spangled Banner. Francis Scott Key.
5. Americans wanted more land for homes and farms.
6. Alaska and Hawaii.
7. The Civil War was a war between the states in the North and the states in the South. From 1861 to 1865.
8. Abraham Lincoln. He wanted to save the Union. / He wanted the Northern and Southern states to stay together. / He was against slavery. / He signed the Emancipation Proclamation.
9. Amendments. Twenty-seven (27).
10. The cotton gin / sewing machine / telephone / typewriter / phonograph / light bulb.
11. Workers had a difficult life. / Their pay was low. / Many workers got hurt because factories weren't safe. / They fought for better hours, better pay, and safer workplaces.
12. The United States needed farmers and workers. / The United States needed people to work on farms and in factories.
13. The American economy collapsed. / Factories closed. / Workers lost their jobs. / Many banks closed. / Many people lost all their money in the stock market.
14. Franklin D. Roosevelt. The government made jobs for people who had no work. / The government gave people loans to help them keep their farms or homes. / The Social Security system began.
15. Germany, Italy, and Japan.
16. An international organization where countries discuss world problems and try to keep peace.
17. The United States and the Soviet Union. The United States has a democratic system of government, and the Soviet Union had a communist system.
18. The civil rights movement worked for equal rights for all Americans. Martin Luther King, Jr.
19. The right to vote.
20. Terrorists hijacked four airplanes and attacked the World Trade Center in New York City and the Pentagon in Arlington, Virginia.

VOICES OF FREEDOM

Student Name
1.
2.
3.
4.
5.
6.
7.
8.
9.
10.
11.
12.
13.
14.
15.
16.
17.
18.
19.
20.

Instructions: Fill in student names on the list mask and affix to Assessment Record sheets.

(cut or fold)

Voices of Freedom
Student Name List Mask

Student Name	Civic Participation	Project Activity	Community Issues
1.			
2.			
3.			
4.			
5.			
6.			
7.			
8.			
9.			
10.			
11.			
12.			
13.			
14.			
15.			
16.			
17.			
18.			
19.			
20.			

Scoring Rubrics:

CIVIC PARTICIPATION Score the student's participation in the discussion:
   5 (Excellent), **4** (Good), **3** (Fair), **2** (Poor), or **1** (Unsatisfactory)

PROJECT ACTIVITY Score **1** (Satisfactory) or **0** (Unsatisfactory) for the student's performance in each of the following:
   Identifying/Assigning Tasks; Accomplishing Assigned Task(s); Leadership; Teamwork; Quality of Final Product.
   (The Project Activity Observation Checklist can be used for scoring this activity.)

COMMUNITY ISSUES Score the student's participation in the discussion:
   5 (Excellent), **4** (Good), **3** (Fair), **2** (Poor), or **1** (Unsatisfactory)

Student Name	Civic Participation	Bulletin Brd. Project	Calendar Project
1.			
2.			
3.			
4.			
5.			
6.			
7.			
8.			
9.			
10.			
11.			
12.			
13.			
14.			
15.			
16.			
17.			
18.			
19.			
20.			

Scoring Rubrics:

CIVIC PARTICIPATION Score the student's participation in the activity as the class circulates around the school and students introduce themselves to school personnel:
5 (Excellent), 4 (Good), 3 (Fair), 2 (Poor), or 1 (Unsatisfactory)

BULLETIN BOARD PROJECT Score 1 (Satisfactory) or 0 (Unsatisfactory) for the student's performance in each of the following: Identifying/Assigning Tasks; Accomplishing Assigned Task(s); Leadership; Teamwork; Quality of Final Product. (The Project Activity Observation Checklist can be used for scoring this activity.)

CALENDAR PROJECT Score 1 (Satisfactory) or 0 (Unsatisfactory) for the student's performance in each of the following: Identifying/Assigning Tasks; Accomplishing Assigned Task(s); Leadership; Teamwork; Quality of Final Product. (The Project Activity Observation Checklist can be used for scoring this activity.)

Student Name	Civic Participation	Project Activity	Community Issues
1.			
2.			
3.			
4.			
5.			
6.			
7.			
8.			
9.			
10.			
11.			
12.			
13.			
14.			
15.			
16.			
17.			
18.			
19.			
20.			

Scoring Rubrics:

CIVIC PARTICIPATION Score the student's participation in the map activity:
5 (Excellent), 4 (Good), 3 (Fair), 2 (Poor), or 1 (Unsatisfactory)

PROJECT ACTIVITY Score 1 (Satisfactory) or 0 (Unsatisfactory) for the student's performance in each of the following:
Identifying/Assigning Tasks; Accomplishing Assigned Task(s); Leadership; Teamwork; Quality of Final Product.
(The Project Activity Observation Checklist can be used for scoring this activity.)

COMMUNITY ISSUES Score the student's participation in the discussion:
5 (Excellent), 4 (Good), 3 (Fair), 2 (Poor), or 1 (Unsatisfactory)

Student Name	Civic Participation	Project Activity	Internet Activity
1.			
2.			
3.			
4.			
5.			
6.			
7.			
8.			
9.			
10.			
11.			
12.			
13.			
14.			
15.			
16.			
17.			
18.			
19.			
20.			

Scoring Rubrics:

CIVIC PARTICIPATION Score the student's participation in the discussion:
5 (Excellent), **4** (Good), **3** (Fair), **2** (Poor), or **1** (Unsatisfactory)

PROJECT ACTIVITY Score **1** (Satisfactory) or **0** (Unsatisfactory) for the student's performance in each of the following: Identifying/Assigning Tasks; Accomplishing Assigned Task(s); Leadership; Teamwork; Quality of Final Product. (The Project Activity Observation Checklist can be used for scoring this activity.)

INTERNET ACTIVITY Score the student's ability to access and navigate the search engine and the student's ability to answer the questions correctly:
5 (Excellent), **4** (Good), **3** (Fair), **2** (Poor), or **1** (Unsatisfactory)

Student Name	Civic Participation	Project Activity	Internet Activity
1.			
2.			
3.			
4.			
5.			
6.			
7.			
8.			
9.			
10.			
11.			
12.			
13.			
14.			
15.			
16.			
17.			
18.			
19.			
20.			

Scoring Rubrics:

CIVIC PARTICIPATION Score the student's participation in the conversation practice:
5 (Excellent), **4** (Good), **3** (Fair), **2** (Poor), or **1** (Unsatisfactory)

COMMUNITY ISSUES Score the student's participation in the discussion:
5 (Excellent), **4** (Good), **3** (Fair), **2** (Poor), or **1** (Unsatisfactory)

INTERNET ACTIVITY Score the student's ability to access and navigate the website and to describe the kind of information it has:
5 (Excellent), **4** (Good), **3** (Fair), **2** (Poor), or **1** (Unsatisfactory)

Student Name	Civic Participation	Internet Activity 1	Internet Activity 2
1.			
2.			
3.			
4.			
5.			
6.			
7.			
8.			
9.			
10.			
11.			
12.			
13.			
14.			
15.			
16.			
17.			
18.			
19.			
20.			

Scoring Rubrics:

CIVIC PARTICIPATION Score the student's participation during the visit with the U.S. representative:
   5 (Excellent), **4** (Good), **3** (Fair), **2** (Poor), or **1** (Unsatisfactory)

INTERNET ACTIVITY 1 Score the student's ability to access and navigate the website and to describe the information provided in the virtual tour of the U.S. Capitol:
   5 (Excellent), **4** (Good), **3** (Fair), **2** (Poor), or **1** (Unsatisfactory)

INTERNET ACTIVITY 2 Score the student's ability to access and navigate the website and to locate and describe the requested information:
   5 (Excellent), **4** (Good), **3** (Fair), **2** (Poor), or **1** (Unsatisfactory)

Student Name	Civic Participation	Project Activity	Community Issues
1.			
2.			
3.			
4.			
5.			
6.			
7.			
8.			
9.			
10.			
11.			
12.			
13.			
14.			
15.			
16.			
17.			
18.			
19.			
20.			

Scoring Rubrics:

CIVIC PARTICIPATION Score the student's participation during the field trip:
5 (Excellent), **4** (Good), **3** (Fair), **2** (Poor), or **1** (Unsatisfactory)

PROJECT ACTIVITY Score **1** (Satisfactory) or **0** (Unsatisfactory) for the student's performance in each of the following: Identifying/Assigning Tasks; Accomplishing Assigned Task(s); Leadership; Teamwork; Quality of Final Product. (The Project Activity Observation Checklist can be used for scoring this activity.)

COMMUNITY ISSUES Score the student's participation in the discussion:
5 (Excellent), **4** (Good), **3** (Fair), **2** (Poor), or **1** (Unsatisfactory)

Student Name	Civic Participation	Project Activity	Internet Activity
1.			
2.			
3.			
4.			
5.			
6.			
7.			
8.			
9.			
10.			
11.			
12.			
13.			
14.			
15.			
16.			
17.			
18.			
19.			
20.			

Scoring Rubrics:

CIVIC PARTICIPATION Score the student's participation during the field trip:
   5 (Excellent), **4** (Good), **3** (Fair), **2** (Poor), or **1** (Unsatisfactory)

PROJECT ACTIVITY Score **1** (Satisfactory) or **0** (Unsatisfactory) for the student's performance in each of the following: Identifying/Assigning Tasks; Accomplishing Assigned Task(s); Leadership; Teamwork; Ability to Share Recipe Instructions with the class. (The Project Activity Observation Checklist can be used for scoring this activity.)

INTERNET ACTIVITY Score the student's ability to access and navigate the website and to locate and describe the information provided in the virtual tour of Plimoth Plantation:
   5 (Excellent), **4** (Good), **3** (Fair), **2** (Poor), or **1** (Unsatisfactory)

VOICES OF FREEDOM

Student Name	Civic Participation	Project Activity	Internet Activity
1.			
2.			
3.			
4.			
5.			
6.			
7.			
8.			
9.			
10.			
11.			
12.			
13.			
14.			
15.			
16.			
17.			
18.			
19.			
20.			

Scoring Rubrics:

CIVIC PARTICIPATION Score the student's participation in gathering the requested information and making the class chart about local government services:
5 (Excellent), 4 (Good), 3 (Fair), 2 (Poor), or 1 (Unsatisfactory)

PROJECT ACTIVITY Score 1 (Satisfactory) or 0 (Unsatisfactory) for the student's performance in each of the following: Identifying/Assigning Tasks; Accomplishing Assigned Task(s); Leadership; Teamwork; Quality of Final Product. (The Project Activity Observation Checklist can be used for scoring this activity.)

INTERENT ACTIVITY Score the student's ability to access and navigate the website and to locate and describe the information provided in the virtual tour of historic Philadelphia:
5 (Excellent), 4 (Good), 3 (Fair), 2 (Poor), or 1 (Unsatisfactory)

Student Name	Civic Participation	Project Activity	Community Issues
1.			
2.			
3.			
4.			
5.			
6.			
7.			
8.			
9.			
10.			
11.			
12.			
13.			
14.			
15.			
16.			
17.			
18.			
19.			
20.			

Scoring Rubrics:

CIVIC PARTICIPATION Score the student's participation in the discussion about rights guaranteed by the 1st Amendment:
5 (Excellent), **4** (Good), **3** (Fair), **2** (Poor), or **1** (Unsatisfactory)

PROJECT ACTIVITY Score **1** (Satisfactory) or **0** (Unsatisfactory) for the student's performance in each of the following: Identifying/Assigning Tasks; Accomplishing Assigned Task(s); Leadership; Teamwork; Quality of Final Product. (The Project Activity Observation Checklist can be used for scoring this activity.)

COMMUNITY ISSUES Score the student's participation in the discussion:
5 (Excellent), **4** (Good), **3** (Fair), **2** (Poor), or **1** (Unsatisfactory)

Student Name	Civic Participation	Debate Activity	Internet Activity
1.			
2.			
3.			
4.			
5.			
6.			
7.			
8.			
9.			
10.			
11.			
12.			
13.			
14.			
15.			
16.			
17.			
18.			
19.			
20.			

Scoring Rubrics:

CIVIC PARTICIPATION Score the student's participation in the small group activity about the U.S. Constitution, including the group's presentation to the class:
   5 (Excellent), **4** (Good), **3** (Fair), **2** (Poor), or **1** (Unsatisfactory)

DEBATE ACTIVITY Score the student's participation in the debate:
   5 (Excellent), **4** (Good), **3** (Fair), **2** (Poor), or **1** (Unsatisfactory)

INTERNET ACTIVITY Score the student's ability to access and navigate the websites and to locate and describe the information provided in the virtual tours:
   5 (Excellent), **4** (Good), **3** (Fair), **2** (Poor), or **1** (Unsatisfactory)

Student Name	Civic Participation	Project Activity	Community Issues
1.			
2.			
3.			
4.			
5.			
6.			
7.			
8.			
9.			
10.			
11.			
12.			
13.			
14.			
15.			
16.			
17.			
18.			
19.			
20.			

Scoring Rubrics:

CIVIC PARTICIPATION Score the student's participation in the discussion about voting and, if possible, the class visit to a polling place:
  5 (Excellent), **4** (Good), **3** (Fair), **2** (Poor), or **1** (Unsatisfactory)

PROJECT ACTIVITY Score the student's biography about a famous American, basing the score on the content and correctness of form of the student's writing:
  5 (Excellent), **4** (Good), **3** (Fair), **2** (Poor), or **1** (Unsatisfactory)

COMMUNITY ISSUES Score the student's participation in the discussion:
  5 (Excellent), **4** (Good), **3** (Fair), **2** (Poor), or **1** (Unsatisfactory)

VOICES OF FREEDOM
Project Activity Observation Checklist

Activity _____

Date _____

Student Name	Identifying/ Assigning Tasks	Accomplishing Assigned Task(s)	Leadership	Teamwork	Quality of Final Product	TOTAL SCORE
1.						
2.						
3.						
4.						
5.						
6.						
7.						
8.						
9.						
10.						
11.						
12.						
13.						
14.						
15.						
16.						
17.						
18.						
19.						
20.						

Scoring Rubric:

Voices of Freedom project activities are intended to serve as a basis for building students' skills in leadership, teamwork, and communicating information—key workplace skills identified by the Secretary's Commission on Achieving Necessary Skills (SCANS). Students should take responsibility for all aspects of the project. Have them identify the particular tasks involved in the project, assign the tasks to different students, gather needed resources, work as a team, and complete the finished product. Use this Project Activity Observation Checklist to evaluate students as you observe them participating in all phases of the project.

Score **1** (Satisfactory) or **0** (Unsatisfactory) for each student's performance in each of the following: Identifying/Assigning Tasks; Accomplishing Assigned Task(s); Leadership; Teamwork; Quality of Final Product.

VOICES OF FREEDOM
Chapter Test Answer Sheet

CHAPTER _____

Student's Name _____ I.D. Number _____

Course _____ Teacher _____ Date _____

A. 1 Ⓐ Ⓑ Ⓒ Ⓓ
    2 Ⓐ Ⓑ Ⓒ Ⓓ
    3 Ⓐ Ⓑ Ⓒ Ⓓ
    4 Ⓐ Ⓑ Ⓒ Ⓓ
    5 Ⓐ Ⓑ Ⓒ Ⓓ
    6 Ⓐ Ⓑ Ⓒ Ⓓ
    7 Ⓐ Ⓑ Ⓒ Ⓓ
    8 Ⓐ Ⓑ Ⓒ Ⓓ
    9 Ⓐ Ⓑ Ⓒ Ⓓ
   10 Ⓐ Ⓑ Ⓒ Ⓓ
   11 Ⓐ Ⓑ Ⓒ Ⓓ
   12 Ⓐ Ⓑ Ⓒ Ⓓ

B. 13 Ⓐ Ⓑ Ⓒ Ⓓ
   14 Ⓐ Ⓑ Ⓒ Ⓓ
   15 Ⓐ Ⓑ Ⓒ Ⓓ
   16 Ⓐ Ⓑ Ⓒ Ⓓ
   17 Ⓐ Ⓑ Ⓒ Ⓓ
   18 Ⓐ Ⓑ Ⓒ Ⓓ
   19 Ⓐ Ⓑ Ⓒ Ⓓ
   20 Ⓐ Ⓑ Ⓒ Ⓓ

C. 1. _____

    2. _____

    3. _____

    4. _____

    5. _____

THE INS INTERVIEW: *Information for Students*

During the INS interview, the examiner will evaluate your ability to read, write, and speak English. The examiner may ask basic questions, such as "How did you get here today?" The examiner may also ask about information on your Form N-400 (Application for Naturalization). You should prepare to talk about the information on your application form. You should especially prepare to talk about any unusual information on your form, such as absences from the United States, selective service registration, taxes, welfare, divorce, and arrests. Here are examples of the types of questions that may occur during the interview:

INTRODUCTION / SWEARING IN

Please raise your right hand. Do you solemnly swear to tell the truth, the whole truth, and nothing but the truth, so help you God?
Please show me your identification / driver's license / permanent resident card (green card).

FORM N-400 PART 1

What's your family name / last name / surname?
What's your given name / first name?
What's your full middle name?
Is your family name / last name / surname _____?
Is your given name / first name _____?
Is your full middle name _____?

Are you changing your name? / Do you want to change your name?
Have you ever used other names?

FORM N-400 PART 2

How long have you lived in the United States? / How long have you been living in the United States? / How long have you been in the United States? / How long have you been a lawful permanent resident of the United States?

FORM N-400 PART 3

What's your social security number?
Is your social security number _____?

What's your date of birth? / What's your birth date? / When were you born?
Is your date of birth _____? / Is your birth date _____? / Were you born on _____?

When did you become a permanent resident? / On what date did you become a permanent resident?

Where were you born? / In what country were you born? / What's your country of birth?
Were you born in _____?

What's your nationality?

Are either of your parents U.S. citizens?

What's your marital status? / What's your current marital status?
Are you single? married? divorced? widowed?

FORM N-400 PART 4

Is your address still _____? / Do you still live at _____? / Are you still living at _____?
Have you changed your address? / Have you moved?
What's your new address?

What's your daytime phone number?
Is your daytime phone number _____?

What's your evening phone number?
Is your evening phone number _____?

FORM N-400 PART 5

What's your height? / How tall are you?

What's your weight? / How much do you weigh?

What's your eye color? / What color are your eyes?

FORM N-400 PART 6

Where do you live now? / What's your current address?
Do you still live at _____? / Is your address still _____? / Are you still living at _____?

Where did you live before that? / What was your previous address? / What was your
address before your current address?
Was your previous address _____?

Are you employed? / Are you working? Where?
Where do you work?
What's the name of your employer? / Who is your employer?
What's your employer's address?
What's your occupation / job / position?
How long have you worked there? / How long have you been working there?
Where did you work before that? / What was your previous job? / What did you do before
that?

FORM N-400 PART 7

Have you been absent from the United States during the past five years? / Have you spent
time outside the United States during the past five years?

How many trips have you taken outside the United States during the past five years? /
How many trips have you taken outside the United States since you became a permanent
resident?

When did you last leave the United States? / When was the last time you left the United
States?
How long were you away / absent / gone?
Where did you go / travel?
Why? / What was the reason for the trip?

FORM N-400 PART 8

How many times have you been married?
Are you married now? / Are you currently married?
When were you married? / What's the date of your marriage?
What's your wife's/husband's/spouse's name?
What's her/his citizenship?
Is she/he a U.S. citizen?
When did she/he become a U.S. citizen?
Is she/he going to apply for citizenship? / Does she/he plan to apply for citizenship?

FORM N-400 PART 9

How many children do you have? / How many sons and daughters have you had?
What are their names?
What is your oldest child's name? How old is she/he?
What are your other children's names? How old are they?
Where were your children born?
Do they live with you now?
Where do they live?

FORM N-400 PART 10

Have you ever claimed to be a U.S. citizen?
Have you ever registered to vote in an election in the United States?
Have you ever voted in an election in the United States?
Have you ever failed to file a federal, state, or local tax return?
Do you owe any federal, state, or local taxes that are overdue?
Do you have any title of nobility in any foreign country?
Have you ever been a patient in a mental institution? / Have you ever been hospitalized for being legally/mentally incompetent?

Have you ever been a member of any organization, association, fund, foundation, party, club, society, or similar group in the United States or in any other place?
What was the name of the group?

Have you ever been a member of the Communist Party?
Have you ever been a member of any other totalitarian party?
Have you ever been a member of any terrorist organization?

Have you ever advocated the overthrow of any government by force or violence?
Have you ever persecuted any person because of race, religion, national origin, membership in a particular social group, or political opinion?
Between March 23, 1933, and May 8, 1945, did you work for or associate in any way with the Nazi government of Germany?

Have you ever called yourself a "nonresident" on a federal, state, or local tax return?
Have you ever failed to file a federal, state, or local tax return because you considered yourself to be a nonresident?

Have you ever committed a crime or offense for which you were not arrested?
Have you ever been arrested?
Have you ever been charged with committing any crime or offense?
Have you ever been convicted of a crime or offense?
Have you ever been in jail or prison?
Explain.

Have you ever been a habitual drunkard? Do you know what that means?
Have you ever been a prostitute or procured anyone for prostitution?
Have you ever sold or smuggled controlled substances, illegal drugs, or narcotics?
Have you ever been married to more than one person at the same time? / Have you ever practiced polygamy?
Have you ever helped anyone enter or try to enter the United States illegally?
Have you ever gambled illegally or received income from illegal gambling?
Have you ever failed to support your dependents or pay alimony?

Have you ever given false information to any U.S. government official?
Have you ever lied to any U.S. government official to gain entry or admission into the United States?
Have you ever been removed, excluded, or deported from the United States?

Have you ever served in the U.S. Armed Forces?
Have you ever left the United States to avoid being drafted into the U.S. Armed Forces?
Have you ever applied for any kind of exemption from military service in the U.S. Armed Forces?
Have you ever deserted from the U.S. Armed Forces?

Have you registered with the Selective Service System?

Do you support the Constitution and form of government of the United States?
Do you understand the full Oath of Allegiance to the United States?
Are you willing to take the full Oath of Allegiance to the United States?
If the law requires it, are you willing to bear arms on behalf of the United States?
If the law requires it, are you willing to perform noncombatant services in the U.S. Armed Forces?
If the law requires it, are you willing to perform work of national importance under civilian direction?

MISCELLANEOUS QUESTIONS

Why do you want to become a citizen?
What are the responsibilities of U.S. citizens?
Are you going to vote when you are a citizen?

How do you like the weather today?

How did you get here today?

Who do you live with?

Do you wish to have an oath ceremony conducted by the INS or in a court? / Where do you wish to have the oath ceremony?

READING TEST

The examiner may ask you to read some of the civics questions, part of the Form N-400, part of the Oath of Allegiance, or some simple sentences.

WRITING TEST

You will be required to write one or more sentences dictated by the examiner.

HISTORY AND GOVERNMENT TEST

The examiner may ask you some questions orally. The examiner may give you some written questions and ask you to read the questions aloud and give the answers. Or the examiner may give you the INS list of 100 questions and ask you to read some questions aloud and give the answers. The examiner might be listening to your answers and reviewing your Form N-400 information at the same time, so don't worry if the examiner isn't looking directly at you while you are answering. If you are reading from a list of questions and you can't answer one, you should say that you don't know the answer and then continue reading and answering the next questions until the examiner says to stop.

ENGLISH & CIVICS INSTRUCTION RESOURCES

ONLINE RESOURCES

These websites can be accessed directly through the Longman English Literacy (EL)/Civics homepage at **http://www.longman.com/ae/elcivics.html**.

http://www.ed.gov/offices/OVAE/AdultEd/ELCIVICS/
EL/Civics homepage, U.S. Department of Education

http://www.ins.usdoj.gov/graphics/services/natz/index.htm
Naturalization homepage, Immigration & Naturalization Service (INS)

http://www.ins.usdoj.gov/graphics/exec/natz/natztest.asp
Naturalization Self-Test, Immigration & Naturalization Service (INS)

http://www.cal.org/ncle/REScivics.htm
Civics Education for Adult English Language Learners, National Center for ESL Literacy Education (NCLE)

http://www.cal.org/ncle/civics/
EL/Civics Activities for Adults, National Center for ESL Literacy Education (NCLE)

http://www.cal.org/ncle/digests/civics.htm
Civics Education for Adult English Language Learners, ERIC Q & A, National Center for ESL Literacy Education (NCLE)

http://www.cal.org/ncle/digests/Needas.htm
Needs Assessment for Adult ESL Learners, ERIC Digest, National Center for ESL Literacy Education (NCLE)

http://hub1.worlded.org/docs/vera/index.htm
Civic Participation and Community Action Sourcebook, New England Literacy Resource Center (Available from World Education, 44 Farnsworth Street, Boston, MA 02210; 617-482-9485)

http://www.nelrc.org/changeagent/backIssues.htm
Civic Participation, downloadable issue of The Change Agent, New England Literacy Resource Center

http://www.pbs.org/literacy/esl/esl.html
ESL CivicsLink homepage, PBS Education Services professional development program

http://www.temple.edu/cil/SHINEhome.htm
Project SHINE (Students Helping In the Naturalization of Elders), Center for Intergenerational Learning, Temple University

http://www-tcall.tamu.edu/newsletr/win02/win02a.htm
English Language Civics: Teaching Beyond Citizenship, Literacy Links, Texas Center for Adult Literacy & Learning

http://www.thecenterweb.org/adult/citizenship.htm
Citizenship homepage, Adult Learning Resource Center, Illinois

http://www.iiri.org/citizenship/
Citizenship preparation student activities, International Institute of Rhode Island

http://www.themlc.org/citizen.htm
Citizenship homepage, Minnesota Literacy Council

VIDEO

Two video programs that present dramatized INS interviews and communication practice:

The INS Interview: Will They Pass?
Alex Alexander, Los Angeles Unified School District
Available from: Vincent B. Kates & Associates, 750 E. Green Street, Suite 301, Pasadena, CA 91101; (626) 793-3944

Citizenship: Success At Your INS Interview
An McDowell, Citizenship Advocacy Project
498 Foam Street, #6, Monterey, CA 93940; (831) 657-0289

Correlation Key

Voices of Freedom	Foundations (Student Book & Workbook)	Word by Word Basic	Word by Word	Side by Side (3rd edition)	Side by Side Interactive CD-ROM / Side by Side TV Video	ExpressWays Book 1 (2nd edition)	Access
Chapter A	Chapter 1	pp. 2–7, 48, 54–55	pp. 1–3, 30, 33	Book 1: Chapters 1–3	Level 1A: Segments 1–4	Chapter 1	Chapters 1, 2
Chapter B	Chapter 1	pp. 2–7, 48, 54–55	pp. 1–3, 30, 33	Book 1: Chapters 4–6	Level 1A: Segments 5–8	Chapter 1	Chapters 3, 4
Chapter 1	Chapter 2	pp. 8–11, 167–171	pp. 4–9	Book 1: Chapters 9, 10	Levels 1A & 1B: Segments 13–15	Chapter 2	
Chapter 2	Chapters 3, 9	pp. 12–17, 98–109	pp. 10–11, 56–61	Book 1: Chapters 7, 8	Level 1A: Segments 9–12	Chapter 4	
Chapter 3	Chapter 4	pp. 18–29, 40–45	pp. 13–18, 25–27	Book 1: Chapter 11	Level 1B: Segments 16, 17	Chapter 3	
Chapter 4	Chapter 5	pp. 52–53, 146–149	pp. 32, 84	Book 1: Chapter 12	Level 1B: Segments 18, 19	Chapter 5	
Chapter 5	Chapter 6	pp. 56–67	pp. 34–39	Book 1: Chapters 13, 14	Level 1B: Segments 20–23	Chapter 5	
Chapter 6	Chapter 8	pp. 76–81	pp. 44–49	Book 1: Chapter 15	Level 1B: Segment 24	Chapter 6	
Chapter 7	Chapter 10	pp. 110–113	pp. 66–67	Book 1: Chapter 16	Level 1B: Segment 25	Chapter 6	
Chapter 8	Chapter 11	pp. 114–127	pp. 68–74	Book 1: Chapter 17	Level 1B: Segment 26	Chapter 7	
Chapter 9	Chapter 12	pp. 128–137	pp. 75–78	Book 2: Chapters 1–3	Level 2A: Segments 27–32	Chapter 7	
Chapter 10	Chapter 13	pp. 138–149	pp. 80–85	Book 2: Chapters 4, 5	Level 2A: Segments 33–36	Chapter 8	

This correlation key indicates textbook lessons that are topically or grammatically related to the instruction in each chapter of *Voices of Freedom* and complement the English and civics curriculum.

Foundations is a pre-beginner's all-skills textbook that offers basic vocabulary and language practice through interactive and communicative activities, games, and exercises.

The **Word by Word Basic** and **Word by Word** Picture Dictionaries present essential words for students' everyday language needs through full-color illustrations and an interactive methodology combining communicative and all-skills practice.

Side by Side is a 4-level textbook series offering all-skills practice through a general language development curriculum based on English grammar and vocabulary.

The **Side by Side Interactive** CD-ROM Program offers interactive exercises that integrate video, audio, graphics, and text and includes check-up tests and lifeskills/civics lessons. The **Side by Side TV** Video Program provides video-based instruction and all-skills practice through accompanying workbooks.

ExpressWays is a 4-level textbook series offering all-skills practice through a competency-based curriculum integrating lifeskills, grammar, and functions of English.

Access, an all-skills text for students with limited literacy skills, offers basic reading and writing practice that supports the instruction provided through the first two chapters of *Voices of Freedom.*